The Personal Papers of
ANTON CHEKHOV

Introduction by MATTHEW JOSEPHSON

Publishers LEAR *New York*

PUBLISHER'S NOTE

The *Notebook* and *Diary* contained in this volume were translated by S. S. Koteliansky and Leonard Woolf. The selection of letters is based on Constance Garnett's *Letters by Anton Chekhov*.

CONTENTS

INTRODUCTION

By Matthew Josephson

For a long period of years it used to be quite the fashion, whenever the subject of Russian national character or Russian literature was broached, to make all sorts of learned allusions to "the mysterious Slavic soul." This form of blague was much in circulation at the turn of the last century when Tolstoy and Dostoevsky were first being discovered by a great public in the West. Toward 1917, however, the stories and plays of Anton Chekhov were at last translated into English in some quantity; it was then we learned that the Russian soul is no more mysterious than the soul of a dweller in the suburbs of London or Brooklyn.

Chekhov was a writer who put forth only modest claims for himself, and was given to brevity and understatement. He had not Tolstoy's great moral certainties, nor the large canvas of Dostoevsky. His songs were short; yet his more than 600 tales and novelettes, by their cumulative effect, provide a *Comédie humaine* of Russian life in their own right.

His world was predominantly that of the middle-class in late nineteenth century Russia; and how much alike are the middle-classes in all lands. In his tales the characters are most commonly troubled intellectuals who talk and talk incessantly about their ideals and their vices, their longings and frustrations. (Did they never go to sleep?) They were men whose will-power often fell short

9

of the hopes or ambitions they had entertained for themselves; they were women fresh from reading the sermons of Ibsen, the New Women whose experiments in social freedom or sexual equality left them touched with disillusionment. For the typical Chekhov tale or play is about people who find themselves in a trap, or a "box" as we nowadays say. There is the woman who hopes to improve her lot by leaving her dull husband and going off with her lover to some resort. The couple who hope that life will be better in the country than in the city; or those "Three Sisters" who plan to escape from the provinces and go to Moscow. But nothing happens, or at least nothing happens as they planned; and the world still seems to make no sense to them They continue to be tormented by their doubts, and above all by the atmosphere of suspense, of waiting for something — which truthfully reflects the era in which Chekhov wrote, in the last decades of Empire Russia, on the eve of the great Revolution.

To read him, then, is to know the background of that Russia which, perhaps needlessly, many Americans have regarded as an enigma. Though Chekhov seems to us one of the most worldly of Russian writers, you feel — especially in his letters — that he is imbued with the deep patriotism that Russians have exhibited for long centuries even in the darkest times of the Tsars. However, this does not prevent him, when traveling abroad, from envying the marked advantages in standard of living or physical comfort enjoyed by West Europeans, as compared even with Russians of the upper class. The scarcity of bathtubs, the dream of *confort moderne*, we perceive, is an old story. In Moscow, as his Notebook relates, when he visits the office of one of the leading literary reviews, he sits down on a sofa that soon yields the cockroach so proverbial in old Russia. Alas, poor Russia! he seems to sigh.

On the other hand, when you study his pictures of the urban working class, or of the peasants, endlessly suffering, only yesterday — as in his novelette, *In the Ravine* — you may measure somewhat the social gains registered since his lifetime, under the Soviet regime. Nor is it surprising that the children of those peasants, in later times, should demonstrate the most tenacious loyalty to the government of Stalin and company.

But Chekhov's Russians of fifty years ago are by no means given over entirely to melancholy; on the contrary, a spirit of utopian optimism often works in them against the counsels of despair. One sees them looking beyond the unhappy present to the hoped-for world of the future, and exclaiming, as in *The Cherry Orchard*, upon "how beautiful, how much better life will be" in later years. A similar faith has been noted in the modern Russians, during recent times of military disaster and mass tragedy. In the same play Chekhov voiced this utopian mood — though in tones of comic pathos that avoided alarming the censor — when he had the student, Trofimov, say prophetically: "We are at least two hundred years behind, we've achieved nothing . . . To begin to live in the present we must first redeem our past, break with it; and we can only expiate it by suffering, by extraordinary, unceasing labor."

The influence of Chekhov on modern writers in England and America has been immense, especially since the years of the first World War. He happened to be translated at a time when interest in applying the more objective modern psychology to literature was at its height; and though he had written chiefly in the 1880's and 1890's, a generation before Marcel Proust and James Joyce came into fashion, the finesse of his analysis caused him to be esteemed as a precursor of those later experts of the subconscious mind. But whereas Joyce, and Proust also, tended to discourage followers; Chekhov's technique appeared deceptively simple and invited widespread imitation.

The appeal of his art lay precisely in its seeming artlessness. Or, as Virginia Woolf said, in "the simplicity, the absence of effort" of his story-telling. He was, to be sure, far from simple. Before Chekhov the masters of the modern short-story were Poe and Maupassant; they wrote stories that had what we used to call plots, and their plots invariably ended with a sharp twist or snap.

Chekhov wrote "stories that had no story," but were great stories. Doubtless he was not the first to try this. The immediate stimulus for his own innovation seems to have come, early in his career, from reading Tolstoy's atmospheric tale of peasant life, "The Death of Ivan Ilyitch." Thereafter Chekhov used systematically the method Tolstoy had employed as if by chance. His stories became as aimless as life itself; they seemed to begin anywhere, rambled, broke off. They ended with a sigh, or a question that was unanswered; or even with the suggestion of a rebeginning (as in *The Lady with the Dog,* or *The Birthday Party*). For whatever may happen to us individually, life goes on as before, does it not?

In all literature there have been few men who have written with such extreme detachment; and because he is so scrupulously objective we tend to accord to Chekhov all the greater rank as a psychologist. Others before Chekhov, even highly "subjective" personalities like Tolstoy, had carried the observation of the human heart to very great depths. But (one simplifies a little) Tolstoy's characters, in comparison, seem more or less solid, monolithic blocks of good *or* evil. Chekhov's personages may be good *and* evil at once; their characters are woven of several strands. Thus in one of his most typical stories, *The Duel,* the two principal male characters, Laevsky and Von Koren, are both wrong-headed; the woman in the picture, Nadezhda, is weakly sinful. But the qualities in them are mixed: we feel their good intentions, their humanity. And we are not surprised because the resolution of their strange conflict is an unexpected one, and by no means conventional tragedy. "We never know all the truth," is the final statement Chekhov leaves us with, in the words of the unhappy Laevsky. The end, as in many of his tales, sets off reverberations within us that continue for some time after the closing lines have been read.

Chekhov knew that he himself was in a box, that with his bad lungs he was fated to die young. But he had great reserves of humor and of human grace that sustained him; his satires are all the more effective because they are compassionate. The world we live in, he seems to say, is heaped with misery, and our chief task is to understand our fellow-sufferers. Not to preach; not to condemn; to understand. The advice he gives to a young writer in one of his letters (to Mme. Avilov, Mar. 19, 1892) illustrates his own approach well: "When you depict sad or unlucky people, and want to touch the reader's heart, try to be colder . . ." In this way, episodes of misfortune or sorrow will stand out with all the greater force.

The notes and correspondence of Chekhov possess the highest interest for us because of his extreme honesty. How often the great writers are given to striking poses, and not least of all the great Russians, from Turgenev down, who made so much of their "sincerity." But Chekhov truly had a horror of anything approaching bombast, and knew how to laugh at himself. He is so entirely, so charmingly unaffected, that to read his letters is to enter into his study and sit down at ease to listen to him.

Some writers are "born," others are "made." Chekhov was a made writer, blessed neither with leisure nor means, who perfected himself by long and arduous effort. To witness that effort, that struggle, as reflected in his notes, but particularly in the range of his letters, is a most valuable experience for the student of Chekhov's craft.

Though he seemed to express himself effortlessly, writing for him was not something ideal; it was work, as well as one could do it; it meant a living. To a literary friend who criticized him for not developing one of his stories with greater depth he answered:

> On my conscience, I would gladly have spent six months over the "Party"; I like taking things easy, and see no attraction in publishing in white-hot haste. I would willingly, with pleasure, with feeling, in a leisurely way, describe the *whole* of my hero . . . It would give me nothing but pleasure, because I like to take pains and dawdle. But what am I to do? I begin a story by September 10th with the thought that I must finish it by October 5th at the latest; if I don't I shall fail the editor and be left without money. I let myself go in the beginning and write with an easy mind; but by the time I get to the middle I begin to grow timid and to fear that my story will be too long . . .

Chekhov, in short, reproaches himself — that is, in his earlier years — because he is forced to write against time, economizing or foreshortening some of his most cherished projects.

Anton Pavlovich Chekhov was born in 1860, in Taganrog, a port on the Black Sea, and was the son of a freed serf who rose to be a general storekeeper. But his father was unlucky in trade; Anton, with his numerous brothers and sisters, knew hunger in childhood; from the age of eleven he worked at all sorts of menial jobs while going to school. He was no less wretched during the long years when he studied at the university to become a doctor of medicine. Religion, he tells us in one of his letters, had been instilled in him chiefly by means of thrashings; he was brought up "to respect rank and kiss the priest's hand, to bow to other people's ideas, to be thankful for each morsel of bread . . . and play the hypocrite to God and Man . . ." His life was to be, in effect, a long struggle to drive out the "serf" within him.

The notion of writing came to him as a way of fending off hunger and also rescuing his ruined family from misery; at first he did jokes, squibs, sketches, hackwork of all sorts for the newspapers. For about ten years he wrote stories that he considered trash, never giving more than a day to each one. Yet he grew, he learned his métier, and one day wrote *The Steppes* and other tales full of the freshness of his talent, that drew the attention of his distinguished contemporaries. Then the Pushkin Prize was awarded to him, and he woke up to find himself famous, though he jested that this was because he managed to deceive the critics, "just as I deceive many people with my face . . ." By then he approached thirty, with health undermined by overwork and poor nourishment; there were but few years left him to exploit the rich vein he had found.

Earlier he had worked against time because of his poverty; now, though his head brimmed with ideas, and his literary standards were more rigorous than before, he worked against death. The surprising thing about his letters is their brave tone and the infrequency of complaint in them. Indeed, his finest works were written in his last years — his dramas, *The Three Sisters* and *The Cherry Orchard*, and such masterly stories as *In the Ravine* — when, as a doctor, he knew how soon the end would come, which it did, in 1904.

Chekhov's characteristic posture was that of the self-effacing observer. A Dostoevsky might produce superb psychological documents drawn from the inexhaustible well of his introspection; Chekhov, on the other hand, loved to "collect" people and case-histories, scores and hundreds of them. With an objectivity somewhat concealed by his gentle and sympathetic manner, he drew people out; he even coaxed them to drop poses and big words and be simple and truthful before him. You see him also in a garden with the aged, though indefatigable Tolstoy and the youthful Maxim Gorky, who describes the scene in his "Recollections." These men spout: Tolstoy, his favorite doctrines of the goodness of peasant life, the evils of science, the aversion of modern women for sex, the virtue of vegetarianism. And Gorky talks social revolution. But Chekhov takes in everything with his fine gray eyes and is silent.

He deeply admired Tolstoy for his genius and his moral leadership. But did Tolstoy observe the real world any longer? Or did he know only Tolstoy? Because of his unwillingness to read a few specialized books on the subject of woman or science or diet, Chekhov reflected afterward, Tolstoy lapsed into the prejudices of an ignorant man. "From the days of my childhood I have believed in progress . . . since the difference between the time when I used to be thrashed and the time when I ceased to be thrashed was tremendous . . . Reason and justice tell me that in electricity and steam there is more love for mankind than there is in charity and abstinence from meat."

In one of his letters Chekhov reflects the belief that in the future literature would go hand in hand with science, in particular with psychology, which absorbed him no less than Dostoevsky. His own contribution, expressive of his temperament, would be a more objective, a more "scientific" observation of nature than his predecessors had achieved as yet — and nature for him meant of course, men and women and their *moeurs.·*

Moreover he had come into the field at a time when the wave of "tendency" literature, produced by Zola, Tolstoy, Ibsen and others, seemed to have reached a crest from which it was soon to recede.

It was against the distortion of truth by the exponents of tendency that Chekhov reacted strongly. They might call themselves realists or naturalists; but they preached, they arranged their slices-of-life in arbitrary patterns to support their doctrines of heretical Christianity or social-ism. And each had his message, his *system* that provided for everything. Chekhov would have no social message. He at least, he promised, would have the honesty, "even the courage to say that he did not understand everything." This alone would be a step forward.

In his Notebook one comes upon such a passage as the following:

> When one is peacefully at home, life seems ordinary, but as soon as one walks into the street and begins to observe, to question women for in-stance, then life becomes terrible. The neighbor-hood of Patriarshi Prudy (a park and street in Moscow) looks quiet and peaceful, but in reality life there is hell.

From such a note evolves the story or novella or play whose pattern Chekhov seeks to fit to the rhythm of every-day-life. These notes, a sentence to a paragraph in length, are really Chekhov tales in miniature. Here for example is the theme of the country estate that is soon to be brought under the hammer:

> There is poverty all around; and the footmen are still dressed like court-jesters.

Was this the germ of *The Cherry Orchard?* Another note mentions two persons whose names are coupled, wrongly, by scandalous gossip about their alleged relations; under the force of suggestion or curiosity they end by trying the experiment of a love affair. One recognizes the theme of one of the author's most ironical stories, *The Grasshopper*, portraying a Russian Mme. Bovary and a bohemian artist, who is drawn after his well-known friend Levitan. (That Chekhov worked directly from the living material around him is shown by the fact that Levitan, on reading the story, dropped over to challenge him for a duel, but was laughed off by Chekhov.)

Since Chekhov's death, early in this century, literature in the hands of its modern exponents has benefited by the most searching technical experiments. One author devotes himself to exploiting the "stream of consciousness"; another the symbolism of ideas; a third the suggestive force of repetition. It is my theory that almost all of these "modern" technical innovations may be found in Chekhov's prose fiction and dramas, *though used with taste and restraint.* This is one of the reasons why so many gifted contemporary writers still hold by him, and in general have not passed beyond the technical limits he marks out.

Literature, as Freud recognized, has always been a reservoir of man's psychological knowledge. There are treasures for the psychiatrist in Shakespeare and in Balzac as in Chekhov. Chekhov quite frequently and deliberately introduced the "internal monologue" into his stories, stripping away his characters to show their double-thinking. (The same device is to be found in Laurence Sterne, in Dickens, as in Stendhal and Dostoevsky.) In Chekhov's *The Birthday Party* the hero habitually poses before everybody and tells little lies for no reason save self-love; he is also shown to be aware of this and filled with bitter disappointment in himself. Yet involuntarily, helplessly, he goes on telling more lies. His wife, a woman of education, observes all his failings and condemns them; but in the midst of her great trials she catches herself at all sorts of poses and deceptions.

Chekhov often introduces dreams into the texture of his stories, repeating the suggestions they carry like a musical theme. In *The Duel* Laevsky's idea that he is an unfortunate representative of the "disillusioned generation" of the '80's is regularly reiterated. In *The Teacher of Literature* a dream, suggesting the sense of inferiority the teacher suffers, haunts the provincial school-teacher. Someone had said to him in scorn: "Then you have never read Lessing?" These words return to him in his dying hour. "There [in the dream] he saw, the oaks and the crows nests like hats. One of the nests rocked; out of it peeped Shebaldin, shouting loudly: "You have not read Lessing?"

But however great his psychological curiosity, or his zest for novelty of form, Chekhov never loses sight of the main business at hand: to communicate to the reader, if not the sense of conventional heroes and villains in conflict, or standard intrigues, the pattern of human existence lived with mounting tension. This is the essential method of his stories as of his plays, whose slow dramatic progression, directed with fine, light strokes, seems to us at once so impalpable and so authentic.

Tolstoy, though his warm friend, reproached him for his lack of "moral focus." Conservatives and liberals alike scolded him for his alleged pessimism. Under the Soviets, since 1917, he has posthumously fluctuated in favor. It is true that he himself sometimes declared that he was unpolitical, attached neither to the Right nor to the Left, but seeking only to be a "free artist . . . who hated lying, violence, stupidity, pharisaism . . . and despotism in all their forms." But was he not, at heart, *engagé* after all; that is, committed to the common struggle? Did not his stories of the manners of polite society constitute a bitter satire of the educated class that should have provided leadership and action? Were not his many tales of lower-class and village life in Russia implicit with indignation and protest at the existing regime — whose censorship he also suffered — and all the stronger for being "coldly" done?

One cannot estimate his moral position fairly without taking into account the epoch in which his formative

years were passed, and to which he makes so many sig-
nificant allusions.   It was once more (!) the time of a
Lost Generation in Russia, that of the 1880's. Following
the liberation of the serfs twenty years earlier, many en-
lightened young Russians had both anticipated and worked
hard for the reform of their political institutions; they had
counted upon the prompt arrival of political democracy,
which reason and justice told them was long overdue.
But with the assassination of Alexander II in 1881, a re-
newed movement of repression drove the liberals under-
ground; their efforts at secret opposition or violence seemed
to bear no fruit thereafter.

Intellectuals like Chekhov, in effect, lived according
to a double standard.   On the one hand they were convinced that the structure of their society was rotten and
their government's policies demented.   On the other hand
they knew that their rulers were all-powerful and they
pretended to conform in order to survive. They were disillusioned, they were unhappy, they waited.   Insofar as
censorship permitted, Chekhov painted accurately the
effects of the social dilemma of his time, the mood of
disillusionment and suspense. The mood is close to that
of our own so-called Lost Generation of the 1920's; it is
close to us again in the late '40's, after a second great war,
when not only Russians but Americans and people everywhere wait for peace, or for One World, while still the
real world we live in moves in directions that defy our
reason.

In such a time, when men discover that they have
waited in vain for some long-promised New Dawn, they

end by crying down all the old slogans and doctrines that
aroused false hopes. Above all, they seem to demand,
give us no more fine rhetoric. Please, no more lies — the
truth, at all costs. It was in such terms that Chekhov,
answering reproaches for his extreme objectivity, or pre-
sumed "indifference to good and evil," pointed to the
transitional character of the era in which he lived, saying
in one of his letters:

> We paint life as it is, and beyond that, even if
> you lashed us with whips, we could not go. We
> have neither immediate nor remote aims. We
> have no politics, we do not believe in revolution,
> we have no God, we are not afraid of ghosts, and
> I personally have no fear even of death and
> blindness.

But at the same time he adds a reflection which is a
warning and a self-accusation:

> He who desires nothing, hopes for nothing,
> and is afraid of nothing, cannot be a [true]
> artist.

There was the peril which his mind saw clearly and
from which, in truth, he saved himself. In his later
stories, in the plays he wrote in his last, sickness-ridden
years, is not all the undertone that of one who desires
and who hopes for something better? "What are we
waiting for here?" the people in *The Three Sisters* say
repeatedly. And in *The Anonymous Story*, though the
hero is pictured as a secret revolutionary who has lost his
faith, he is driven to exclaim also: "We suffer so much!"
But since nothing is without purpose in this world, he

adds, surely something must come of this; those who come after us will profit by our experience and our suffering.

Before his end Chekhov's political conscience declared itself more openly than before. During a visit to France, in 1898, he wrote letters home championing Dreyfus and Zola, symbols of a most unpopular cause in official Russian circles. For this his friend of long standing, the powerful publisher Souvorin, rebuked him, and Chekhov severed their friendship. Later he chose to resign from the Academy, when his young friend Gorky was expelled, a gesture that was widely understood.

Chekhov saw finally that time was running out for the old imperial regime, and prophesied an irresistible movement of revolution led, or dominated, by men quite different from those who had long talked about its coming. The future might be nothing like that which the old generation of intellectuals had dreamed; and they, he guessed shrewdly, might be the first to revile it:

> It seems to me, that while we worn-out banal intellectuals are rummaging among old rubbish, and, according to the old Russian custom, biting one another, there is boiling up around us a life which we neither know nor notice. Great events will take us unawares . . .

ANTON CHEKHOV'S NOTEBOOK

1892 - 1904

THE NOTEBOOK

1892 - 1904

MANKIND has conceived history as a series of battles; hitherto it has considered fighting as the main thing in life.

Solomon made a great mistake when he asked for wisdom.[1]

Ordinary hypocrites pretend to be doves; political and literary hypocrites pretend to be eagles. But don't be disconcerted by their aquiline appearance. They are not eagles, but rats or dogs.

Those who are more stupid and more dirty than we are called the people. The administration classifies the population into tax-payers and non-taxpayers. But

---

1 Among Chekhov's papers the following monologue was found, written in his own hand:

Solomon (alone): Oh! how dark is life! No night, when I was a child, so terrified me by its darkness as does my invisible existence. Lord, to David my father thou gavest only the gift of harmonizing words and sounds, to sing and praise thee on strings, to lament sweetly, to make people weep or admire beauty; but why hast thou given me a meditative, sleepless, hungry mind? Like an insect born of the dust, I hide in darkness; and in fear and despair, all shaking and shivering, I see and hear in everything an invisible mystery. Why this morning? Why does the sun come out from behind the temple and gild the palm tree? Why this beauty of women? Where does the bird hurry, what is the meaning of its flight, if it and its young and the place to which it hastens will, like myself, turn to dust? It were better I had never been born or were a stone, to which God has given neither eyes nor thoughts. In order to tire out my body by nightfall, all day yesterday, like a mere workman I carried marble to the temple; but now the night has come and I cannot sleep . . . I'll go and lie down. Phorses told me that if one imagines a flock of sheep running and fixes one's attention upon it, the mind gets confused and one falls asleep. I'll do it. . . . (exit).

27

neither classification will do; we are all the people and all the best we are doing is the people's work.

If the Prince of Monaco has a roulette table, surely convicts may play at cards.

Iv. (Chekhov's brother Ivan) could philosophize about love, but he could not love.
Aliosha: "My mind, mother, is weakened by illness and I am now like a child: now I pray to God, now I cry, now I am happy."

Why did Hamlet trouble about ghosts after death, when life itself is haunted by ghosts so much more terrible?

Daughter: "Felt boots are not the correct thing."
Father: "Yes they are clumsy, I'll have to get leather ones." The father fell ill and his deportation to Siberia was postponed.
Daughter: "You are not at all ill, father. Look, you have your coat and boots on. . . ."
Father: "I long to be exiled to Siberia. One could sit somewhere by the Yenissei or Ob river and fish, and on the ferry there would be nice little convicts, emigrants. . . . Here I hate everything: this lilac tree in front of the window, these gravel paths. . . ."

A bedroom. The light of the moon shines so brightly through the window that even the buttons on his night shirt are visible.

A nice man would feel ashamed even before a dog. . . .

A certain Councillor of State, looking at a beautiful landscape, said: "What a marvelous function of nature!" From the note-book of an old dog: "People don't eat slops and bones which the cooks throw away. Fools!"

He had nothing in his soul except˙recollections of his schooldays.

The French say: "Laid comme un chenille" — as ugly as a caterpillar.

People are bachelors or old maids because they rouse no interest, not even a physical one.

The children growing up talked at meals about religion and laughed at fasts, monks, etc. The old mother at first lost her temper, then, evidently getting used to it, only smiled, but at last she told the children that they had convinced her, that she is now of their opinion. The children felt awkward and could not imagine what their old mother would do without her religion.

There is no national science, just as there is no national multiplication table; what is national is no longer science.

The dog walked in the street and was ashamed of its crooked legs.

The difference between man and woman: a woman, as she grows old gives herself up more and more to female affairs; a man, as he grows old, withdraws himself more and more from female affairs.

That sudden and ill-timed love-affair may be compared to this: you take boys somewhere for a walk; the walk is jolly and interesting — and suddenly one of them gorges himself with oil paint.

The character in the play says to every one: "You've got worms." He cures his daughter of the worms, and she turns yellow.

A scholar, without talent, a blockhead, worked for twenty-four years and produced nothing good, gave the world only scholars as untalented and as narrow-minded as himself. At night he secretly bound books — that was his true vocation: in that he was an artist and felt the joy of it. There came to him a bookbinder, who loved learning and studied secretly at night.

But perhaps the universe is suspended on the tooth of some monster.

Keep to the right, you of the yellow eye!

Do you want to eat?
No, on the contrary.

A pregnant woman with short arms and a long neck, like a kangaroo.

How pleasant it is to respect people! When I see books,

I am not concerned with how the authors loved or played cards; I see only their marvelous works.

To demand that the woman who loves should be pure is egotistical: to look for that in a woman which I have not got myself is not love, but worship, since one ought to love one's equals.

The so-called pure childlike joy of life is animal joy.

I cannot bear the crying of children, but when my child cries, I don't hear.

A schoolboy treats a lady to dinner in a restaurant. He has only one rouble, twenty kopecks. The bill comes to four roubles thirty kopecks. He has no money and begins to cry. The proprietor boxes his ears. He was talking to the lady about Abyssinia.

A man, who, to judge from his appearance, loves nothing but sausages and sauerkraut.

We judge human activities by their goal; that activity is great of which the goal is great.

You drive on the Nevski, you look to the left on the Haymarket; the clouds are the color of smoke, the ball of the setting sun purple — Dante's hell!

His income is twenty-five to fifty thousand, and yet out of poverty he shoots himself.

Terrible poverty, desperate situation. The mother a widow, her daughter a very ugly girl. At last the mother takes courage and advises the daughter to go on the streets. She herself when young went on the streets without her husband's knowledge in order to get money for her dresses; she has some experience. She instructs her daughter. The latter goes out, walks all night; not a single man takes her; she is ugly. A couple of days later, three young rascals on the boulevard take her. She brought home a note which turned out to be a lottery ticket no longer valid.

Two wives: one in Petersburg, the other in Kerch. Constant rows, threats, telegrams. They nearly reduce him to suicide. At last he finds a way: he settles them both in the same house. They are perplexed, petrified; they grow silent and quiet down.

His character is so undeveloped that one can hardly believe that he has been to the University.

And I dreamt that, as it were, what I considered reality was a dream, and the dream was reality.

I observed that after marriage people cease to be curious.

It usually takes as much time to feel happy as to wind up one's watch.

A dirty tavern near the station. And in every tavern like that you will find salted white sturgeon with horse radish. What a lot of sturgeon must be salted in Russia!

Z. goes on Sundays to the Sukharevka (a market-place in Moscow) to look for books; he finds a book, written by his father, with the inscription: "To darling Nadya from the author."

A Government official wears on his chest the portrait of the Governor's wife; he feeds a turkey on nuts and makes her a present of it.

One should be mentally clear, morally pure, and physically tidy.

It was said of a certain lady that she had a cat's factory; her lover tortured the cats by treading on their tails.

An officer and his wife went to the baths together, and both were bathed by the orderly, whom they evidently did not consider a man.

"And now he appeared with all his decorations."
"And what decorations has he got?"
"He has a bronze medal for the census of 1897."

A government clerk gave his son a thrashing because he had only obtained five marks in all his subjects at school. It seemed to him not good enough. When he was told that he was in the wrong, that five is the highest mark obtainable, he thrashed his son again — out of vexation with himself.

A very good man has such a face that people take him for a detective; he is suspected of having stolen shirt-studs.

A serious phlegmatic doctor fell in love with a girl who danced very well, and, to please her, he started to learn a mazurka.

The hen sparrow believes that her cock sparrow is not chirping but singing beautifully.

When one is peacefully at home, life seems ordinary, but as soon as one walks into the street and begins to observe, to question women, for instance, then life becomes terrible. The neighborhood of Patriarshi Prudy (a park and street in Moscow) looks quiet and peaceful, but in reality life there is hell.

These red-faced young and old women are so healthy that steam seems to exhale from them.

The estate will soon be brought under the hammer; there is poverty all around; and the footmen are still dressed like jesters.

There has been an increase not in the number of nervous diseases and nervous patients, but in the number of doctors able to study those diseases.

The more refined the more unhappy.

Life does not agree with philosophy: there is no happiness which is not idleness and only the useless is pleasurable.

The grandfather is given fish to eat, and if it does not poison him and he remains alive, then all the family eat it.

A correspondence.   A young man dreams of devoting himself to literature and constantly writes to his father about it; at last he gives up the civil service, goes to Petersburg, and devotes himself to literature — he becomes a censor.

First class sleeping car.   Passengers numbers 6, 7, 8 and 9.   They discuss daughters-in-law.   Simple people suffer from mothers-in-law, intellectuals from daughters-in-law.

"My elder son's wife is educated, arranges Sunday schools and libraries, but she is tactless, cruel, capricious, and physically revolting.   At dinner she will suddenly go off into sham hysterics because of some article in the newspaper.   An affected thing."   Another daughter-in-law: "In society she behaves passably, but at home she is a dolt, smokes, is miserly, and when she drinks tea, she keeps the sugar between her lips and teeth and speaks at the same time."

Miss Mieschankina.

In the servants' quarters Roman, a more or less dissolute peasant, thinks it his duty to look after the morals of the women servants.

A large fat barmaid — a cross between a pig and white sturgeon.

At Malo-Bronnaya (a street in Moscow). A little girl who has never been in the country feels it and raves about it, speaks about jackdaws, crows and colts, imagining parks and birds on trees.

Two young officers in stays.

A certain captain taught his daughter the art of fortification.   .

New literary forms always produce new forms of life and that is why they are so revolting to the conservative human mind.

A neurasthenic undergraduate comes home to a lonely country-house, reads French monologues, and finds them stupid.

People love talking of their diseases, although they are the most uninteresting things in their lives.

An official, who wore the portrait of the Governor's wife, lent money on interest; he secretly becomes rich. The late Governor's wife, whose portrait he has worn for fourteen years, now lives in a suburb, a poor widow; her son gets into trouble and she needs 4,000 roubles. She goes to the official, and he listens to her with a bored look and says: "I can't do anything for you, my lady."

Women deprived of the company of men pine, men deprived of the company of women become stupid.

A sick innkeeper said to the doctor: "If I get ill, then for the love of God come without waiting for a summons. My sister will never call you in, whatever happens; she is a miser, and your fee is three roubles a visit." A month or two later the doctor heard that the innkeeper was seriously ill, and while he was making his preparations to go and see him, he received a letter from the sister saying: "My brother is dead." Five days later the doctor happened to go to the village and was told there that the innkeeper had died that morning. Disgusted he went to the inn. The sister dressed in black stood in the corner reading a psalm book. The doctor began to upbraid her for her stinginess and cruelty. The sister went on reading the psalms, but between every two sentences she stopped to quarrel with him — "Lots of your like running about here. . . . The devils brought you here." She belongs to the old faith, hates passionately and swears desperately.

The new governor made a speech to his clerks. He called the merchants together — another speech. At the annual prize-giving of the secondary school for girls — a speech on true enlightenment. To the representatives of the press a speech. He called the Jews together: "Jews, I have summoned you.". . . A month or two passes — he does nothing. Again he calls the merchants together — a speech. Again the Jews: "Jews, I have summoned you.". . . He has wearied them all. At last he says to his Chancellor: "No, the work is too much for me, I shall have to resign."

A student at a village theological school was learning Latin by heart. Every half-hour he runs down to the maids' room and, closing his eyes, feels and pinches them; they scream and giggle; he returns to his book again. He calls it "refreshing oneself."

The Governor's wife invited an official, who had a thin voice and was her adorer, to have a cup of chocolate with her, and for a week afterwards he was in bliss. He had saved money and lent it but not on interest. "I can't lend you any, your son-in-law would gamble it away. No, I can't." The son-in-law is the husband of the daughter who once sat in a box in a boa; he lost at cards and embezzled Government money. The official, who was accustomed to herring and vodka, and who had never before drunk chocolate, felt sick after the chocolate. The expression on the lady's face: "Aren't I a darling?"; she spent any amount of money on dresses and looked forward to making a display of them — so she gave parties.

Going to Paris with one's wife is like going to Tula[1] with one's samovar.

The young do not go in for literature, because the best of them work on steam engines, in factories, in industrial undertakings. All of them have now gone into industry, and industry is making enormous progress.

Families where the woman is bourgeoise easily breed adventurers, swindlers, and brutes without ideals.

---

1 Tula is a Russian city where samovars are manufactured.

A professor's opinion: not Shakespeare, but the commentaries on him are the thing.

Let the coming generation attain happiness; but they surely ought to ask themselves, for what did their ancestors live and for what did they suffer.

Love, friendship, respect do not unite people as much as common hatred for something.

13th December. I saw the owner of a mill, the mother of a family, a rich Russian woman, who has never seen a lilac bush in Russia.

In a letter: "A Russian abroad, if not a spy, is a fool." The neighbor goes to Florence to cure himself of love, but at a distance his love grows stronger.

Yalta. A young man, interesting, liked by a lady of forty. He is indifferent to her, avoids her. She suffers and at last, out of spite, gets up a scandal about him.

Pete's mother even in her old age beaded her eyes.

Viciousness is a bag with which man is born.

B. said seriously that he is the Russian Maupassant. And so did S.

A Jewish surname: Cap.

A lady looking like a fish standing on its head; her mouth like a slit, one longs to put a penny in it.

Russians abroad: the men love Russia passionately, but the women don't like her and soon forget her.

Chemist Propter.

Rosalie Ossipovna Aromat.

It is easier to ask of the poor than of the rich.

And she began to engage in prostitution, got used to sleeping on the bed, while her aunt, fallen into poverty, used to lie on the little carpet by her side and jumped up each time the bell rang; when they left, she would say mindingly, with a pathetic grimace: "Something for the chamber-maid." And they would tip her sixpence.

Prostitutes in Monte Carlo, the whole tone is prostitutional; the palm trees, it seems, are prostitutes, and the chickens are prostitutes.

A big dolt, Z., a qualified nurse, of the Petersburg Rozhdestvensky School, having ideals, fell in love with X., a teacher, and believed him to be ideal, a public spirited worker after the manner of novels and stories of which she was so fond. Little by little she found him out, a drunkard, an idler, good-natured and not very clever. Dismissed, he began to live on his wife, sponged on her. He was an excrescence, a kind of sarcoma, who wasted her completely. She was once engaged to attend some intellectual country people, she went to them every day; they felt it awkward to give her money — and, to her great vexation, gave her husband a suit as a present. He would drink tea for hours and this infuriated her. Living with her husband she grew thin, ugly, spiteful, stamped her foot and shouted at him: "Leave me, you low fellow." She hated him. She worked, and people paid the money to him, for, being a Zemstvo worker, she took no money, and it enraged her that their friends did not understand him and thought him ideal.

A young man made a million marks, lay down on them, and shot himself.

"That woman.". . . . "I married when I was twenty; I have not drunk a glass of vodka all my life, haven't smoked a single cigarette." After he had run off with another woman, people got to like him more and to believe him more, and, when he walked in the street, he began to notice that they had all become kinder and nicer to him — because he had fallen.

A man and woman marry because both of them don't know what to do with themselves.

The power and salvation of a people lie in its intelligentsia, in the intellectuals who think honestly, feel, and can work.

A man without a mustache is like a woman with a mustache.

A man who cannot win a woman by a kiss will not win her by a blow.

For one sensible person there are a thousand fools, and for one sensible word there are a thousand stupid ones; the thousand overwhelms the one, and that is why cities and villages progress so slowly. The majority, the mass, always remain stupid; it will always overwhelm; the sensible man should give up hope of educating and lifting it up to himself; he had better call in the assistance of material force, build railways,, telegraphs, telephones — in that way he will conquer and help life forward.

Really decent people are only to be found amongst men who have definite, either conservative or radical, convictions; so-called moderate men are much inclined to rewards, commissions, orders, promotions.

"What did your uncle die of?"
"Instead of fifteen Botkin drops,[1] as the doctor prescribed, he took sixteen."

A young philologist, who has just left the University, comes home to his native town. He is elected churchwarden. He does not believe in God, but goes to church regularly, makes the sign of the cross when passing near a church or chapel, thinking that that sort of thing is necessary for the people and that the salvation of Russia is bound up with it. He is elected chairman of the Zemstvo board and a Justice of the Peace, he wins orders and medals; he does not notice that he has reached the age of forty-five; then suddenly he realizes that all the

---

1 A very harmless purgative.

time he has been acting and making a fool of himself, but it is now too late to change his way of life.   Once in his sleep he suddenly hears like the report of a gun the words: "What are you doing?" — and he starts up all in a sweat.

One cannot resist evil, but one can resist good.

He flatters the authorities like a priest.

Instead of sheets — dirty tablecloths.

A Jewish surname: Perchik (little pepper).

A man in conversation: "And all the rest of it."

A rich man, usually insolent, his conceit enormous, but bears his riches like a cross.   If the ladies and generals did not dispense charity on his account, if it were not for the poor students and the beggars, he would feel the anguish of loneliness.   If the beggars struck and agreed not to beg from him, he would go to them himself.

The husband invites his friends to his country-house in the Crimea, and afterwards his wife, without her husband's knowledge, brings them the bill and is paid for board and lodging.

Potapov becomes attached to the brother, and this is the beginning of his falling in love with the sister.   Divorces his wife.   Afterwards the son sends him plans for a rabbit-hutch.

"I have sown clover and oats."

"No good; you had much better sow lucerne."

"I have begun to keep a pig."

"No good. It does not pay. You had better go in for mares."

A girl, a devoted friend, out of the best of motives, went about with a subscription list for X., who was not in want.

Why are the dogs of Constantinople so often described?

Disease: "He has got hydropathy."

I visit a friend, find him at supper; there are many guests. It is very gay; I am glad to chatter with the women and drink wine. A wonderfully pleasant mood. Suddenly up gets N. with an air of importance, as though he were a public prosecutor, and makes a speech in my honor. "The magician of words . . . ideals . . . in our time when ideals grow dim . . . you are sowing wisdom, undying things. . . ." I feel as if I had had a cover over me and that now the cover had been taken off and some one was aiming a pistol at me.

After the speech — a murmur of conversation, then silence. The gayety has gone. "You must speak now," says my neighbor. But what can I say? I would gladly throw the bottle at him. And I go to bed with some sediment in my soul. "Look what a fool sits among you!"

The maid, when she makes the bed, always puts the

slippers under the bed close to the wall. The fat master, unable to bear it any longer, gives the maid notice. It turns out that the doctor told her to put the slippers as far as possible under the bed so as to cure the man of his obesity.

The club blackballed a respectable man because all of the members were out of humor; they ruined his prospects.

A large factory. The young employer plays the superior to all and is rude to the employees who have University degrees. Only the gardener, a German, has the courage to be offended: "How dare you, gold bag?"

A tiny little schoolboy with the name of Trachtenbauer.

Whenever he reads in the newspaper about the death of a great man, he wears mourning.   •

In the theatre. A gentleman asks a lady to take her hat off, as it is in his way. Grumbling, disagreeableness, entreaties. At last a confession: "Madam, I am the author of the play." She answered: "I don't care."

In order to act wisely it is not enough to be wise (Dostoevsky).

A. and B. have a bet. A. wins the wager, by eating twelve cutlets; B. does not pay even for the cutlets.

It is terrible to dine every day with a person who stammers and says stupid things.

Glancing at a plump, appetizing woman: "It is not a woman, it is a full moon."

From her face one would imagine that under her stays she has got gills.

For a farce: Kapiton Ivanovitch Boil.

An income-tax inspector and an excise official, in order to justify their occupations to themselves, say spontaneously: "It is an interesting profession, there is a lot of work, it is a live occupation."

At twenty she loved Z., at twenty-four she married N. not because she loved him, but because she thought him a good, wise, ideal man. The couple lived happily; every one envies them, and indeed their life passes smoothly and placidly; she is satisfied, and, when people discuss love, she says that for family life not love nor passion is wanted, but affection. But once the music played suddenly, and, inside her heart, everything broke up like ice in spring: she remembered Z. and her love for him, and she thought with despair that her life was ruined, spoilt forever, and that she was unhappy. Then it happened to her with the New Year greetings; when people wished her "New Happiness," she indeed longed for new happiness.

Z. goes to a doctor, who examines him and finds that he is suffering from heart disease. Z. abruptly changes his way of life, takes medicine, can only talk about his disease; the whole town knows that he has heart disease

and all the doctors, whom he regularly consults, say that
he has got heart disease. He does not marry, gives up
amateur theatricals, does not drink, and when he walks
does so slowly and hardly breathes. Eleven years later
he has to go to Moscow and there he consults a specialist.
The latter finds that his heart is perfectly sound. Z. is
overjoyed but he can no longer return to a normal life,
for he has got accustomed to going to bed early and to
walking slowly, and he is bored if he cannot speak of his
disease. The only result is that he gets to hate doctors —
that is all.

A woman is fascinated not by art, but by the noise made
by those who have to do with art.

N., a dramatic critic, has a mistress X., an actress. Her
benefit night. The play is rotten, the acting poor, but
N. has to praise. He writes briefly: "The play and the
leading actress had an enormous success. Particulars to-
morrow." As he wrote the last two words, he gave a sigh
of relief. Next day he goes to X.; she opens the door,
allows him to kiss and embrace her, and in a cutting tone
says: "Particulars to-morrow."

In Kislovodsk or some other watering-place Z. picked
up a girl of twenty-two; she was poor, straightforward, he
took pity on her and, in addition to her fee, he left twenty-
five roubles on the chest of drawers; he left her room with
the feeling of a man who has done a good deed. The
next time he visited her, he noticed an expensive ash-

tray and a man's fur cap, bought out of his twenty-five roubles — the girl again starving, her cheeks hollow.

N. mortgages his estate with the Bank of the Nobility at 4 per cent, and then lends the money on mortgage at 12 per cent.

Aristocrats? The same ugly bodies and physical uncleanliness, the same toothless old age and disgusting death, as with market-women.

N., when a group is being photographed, always stands in the front row; on addresses he always signs the first; at anniversaries he is always the first to speak. Always wonders: "O soup! O pastries!"

Z. got tired of having visitors, and he hired a French woman to live in his house as if she were his mistress. This shocked the ladies and he no longer had visitors.

Z. is a torch-bearer at funerals. He is an idealist. "In the undertaker's shop."

N. and Z. are intimate friends, but when they meet in society, they at once make fun of one another — out of shyness.

Complaint: "My son Stepan was delicate, and I therefore sent him to school in the Crimea, but there he was caned with a vinebranch, and that gave him philoxera in the behind and now the doctors can not cure him."

Mitya and Katya were told that their papa blasted rocks in the quarry. They wanted to blow up their cross grand-papa, so they took a pound of powder from their father's room, put it in a bottle, inserted a wick, and placed it under their grandfather's chair, when he was dozing after dinner; but soldiers marched by with the band play-ing — and this was the only thing that prevented them from carrying out their plan.

Sleep is a marvelous mystery of Nature which renews all the powers of man, bodily and spiritual. (Bishop Porphyrius Usgensky, "The Book of My Life.")

A woman imagines that she has a peculiar, exceptional constitution, whose ailments are different from other people's and which cannot stand ordinary medicine. She thinks that her son is unlike other people's sons, that he has to be brought up differently. She believes in princi-ples, but she thinks that they apply to every one but her-self, because she lives in exceptional circumstances. The son grows up, and she tries to find an exceptional wife for him. Those around her suffer. The son turns out a scoundrel.

Poor long-suffering art!

A man whose madness takes the form of an idea that he is a ghost: walks at night.

A sentimental man, like Lavrov, has moments of

pleasant emotion and makes the request: "Write a letter to my auntie in Briansk; she is a darling. . . ."

There is a bad smell in the barn: ten years ago haymakers slept the night in it and ever since it smells.

An officer at a doctor's. The money on a plate. The doctor can see in the looking-glass that the patient takes twenty-five roubles from the plate and pays him with it.

Russia is a nobody's country!

Z. who is always saying banal things: "With the agility of a bear," "on one's favorite corn."

A savings bank: the clerk, a very nice man, looks down on the bank, considers it useless — and yet goes on working there.

A radical lady, who crosses herself at night, is secretly full of prejudice and superstition, hears that in order to be happy one should boil a black cat by night. She steals a cat and tries to boil it.

A publisher's twenty-fifth anniversary. Tears, a speech: "I offer ten roubles to the literary fund, the interest to be paid to the poorest writer, but on condition that a special committee is appointed to work out the rules according to which the distribution shall be made."

He wore a blouse and despised those who wore frock coats. A stew of trousers.

The ice cream is made of milk in which, at it were, the patients bathed.

It was a grand forest of timber, but a Government Conservator was appointed, and in two years time there was no more timber; the caterpillar pest.

X.: "Choleraic disorder in my stomach started with the cider."

Of some writers each work taken separately is brilliant, but taken as a whole they are indefinite; of others each particular work represents nothing outstanding; but, for all that, taken as a whole they are distinct and brilliant.

N. rings at the door of an actress; he is nervous, his heart beats, at the critical moment he gets into a panic and runs away; the maid opens the door and sees nobody. He returns, rings again — but has not the courage to go in. In the end the porter comes out and gives him a thrashing.

A gentle quiet schoolmistress secretly beats her pupils, because she believes in the good of corporal punishment.

N.: "Not only the dog, but even the horses howled."

N. marries. His mother and sister see a great many faults in his wife; they are distressed, and only after four or five years realize that she is just like themselves.

The wife cried. The husband took her by the shoulders and shook her, and she stopped crying.

After his marriage everything — politics, literature, society — did not seem to him as interesting as they had before; but now every trifle concerning his wife and child became a most important matter.

"Why are thy songs so short?" a bird was once asked. "Is it because thou art short of breath?"

"I have very many songs and I should like to sing them all."

(A. Daudet.)

The dog hates the teacher; they tell it not to bark at him; it looks, does not bark, only whimpers with rage.

Faith is a spiritual faculty; animals have not got it; savages and uncivilized people have merely fear and doubt. Only highly developed natures can have faith.

Death is terrible, but still more terrible is the feeling that you might live forever and never die.

The public really loves in art that which is banal and long familiar, that to which they have grown accustomed.

A progressive, educated, young, but stingy school guardian inspects the school every day, makes long speeches there, but does not spend a penny on it: the school is falling to pieces, but he considers himself useful and necessary. The teacher hates him, but he does not notice it. The harm is great. Once the teacher, unable to stand it any longer, facing him with anger and disgust, bursts out swearing at him.

Teacher: "Pushkin's centenary should not be celebrated; he did nothing for the church."

Miss Guitarov (actress).

If you wish to become an optimist and understand life, stop believing what people say and write, observe and discover for yourself.

Husband and wife zealously followed X.'s idea and built up their life according to it as if it were a formula. Only just before death they asked themselves: "Perhaps that idea is wrong? Perhaps the saying 'mens sana in corpore sano' is untrue?

I detest: a playful Jew, a radical Ukrainian, and a drunken German.

The University brings out all abilities, including stupidity.

Taking into consideration, dear sir, as a result of this view, dear sir. . . .

The most intolerable people are provincial celebrities.

Owing to our flightiness, because the majority of us are unable and unaccustomed to think or to look deeply into life's phenomena, nowhere else do people so often say: "How banal!" nowhere else do people regard so superficially, and often contemptuously other people's merits or serious questions. On the other hand nowhere else does the authority of a name weigh so heavily as with us Russians, who have been abased by centuries of slavery and fear freedom. . . .

A doctor advised a merchant to eat soup and chicken. The merchant thought the advice ironical. At first he ate a dinner of botvinia and pork, and then, as if recollecting the doctor's orders, ordered soup and chicken and swallowed them down too, thinking it a great joke.

Father Epaminond catches fish and puts them in his pocket; then, when he gets home, he takes out a fish at a time, as he wants it, and fries it.

The nobleman X. sold his estate to N. with all the furniture according to an inventory, but he took away everything else, even the oven dampers, and after that N. hated all noblemen.

The rich, intellectual X., of peasant origin, implored his son: "Mike, don't get out of your class. Be a peasant until you die, do not become a nobleman, nor a merchant, nor a bourgeois. If, as you say, the Zemstvo officer now has the right to inflict corporal punishment on peasants, then let him also have the right to punish you."

He was proud of his peasant origin, he was even haughty about it.

They celebrated the birthday of an honest man. Took the opportunity to show off and praise one another. Only towards the end of the dinner they suddenly discovered that the man had not been invited; they had forgotten.

A gentle quiet woman, getting into a temper says: "If I were a man, I would just bash your filthy mug."

A Mussulman for the salvation of his soul digs a well. It would be a pleasant thing if each of us left a school, a well, or something like that, so that life should not pass away into eternity without leaving a trace behind it.

We are tired out by servility and hypocrisy.

N. once had his clothes torn by dogs, and now, when he pays a call anywhere, he asks: "Aren't there any dogs here?"

A young pimp, in order to keep up his powers, always eats garlic.

School guardian. Widowed priest plays the harmonium and sings: "Rest with the saints."

In July the red bird sings the whole morning.

"A large selection of *cigs*" [1] — so read X. every day when

_____

1 *Cigs* in Russian is a kind of fish.

he went down the street, and wondered how one could deal only in *cigs* and who wanted them. It took him thirty years before he read it correctly: "A large selection of cigars."

A bride to an engineer: a dynamite cartridge filled with one-hundred-rouble notes.

"I have not read Herbert Spencer. Tell me his subjects. What does he write about?" "I want to paint a panel for the Paris exhibition. Suggest a subject." (A wearisome lady.)

The idle, so-called governing, classes cannot remain long without war. When there is no war they are bored, idleness fatigues and irritates them, they do not know what they live for; they bite one another, try to say unpleasant things to one another, if possible with impunity, and the best of them make the greatest efforts not to bore the others and themselves. But when war comes, it possesses all, takes hold of the imagination, and the common misfortune unites all.

An unfaithful wife is a large cold cutlet which one does not want to touch, because some one else has had it in his hands.

An old maid writes a treatise: "The tramline of piety."

Ryzeborsky, Tovbin, Gremoukhin, Koptin.

She had not sufficient skin on her face; in order to open her eyes she had to shut her mouth and *vice versa*.

When she raises her skirt and shows her lace petticoat, it is obvious that she dresses like a woman who is accustomed to be seen by men.

X. philosophizes: "Take the word 'nose.' In Russia it seems something unmentionable, means the deuce knows what, one may say, the indecent part of the body, and in French it means wedding." And indeed X.'s nose was an indecent part of the body.

A girl, flirting, chatters: "All are afraid of me . . . men, and the wind . . . ah, leave me alone! I shall never marry." And at home poverty, her father a regular drunkard. And if people could see how she and her mother work, how she screens her father, they would feel the deepest respect for her and would wonder why she is so ashamed of poverty and work, and is not ashamed of that chatter.

A restaurant. An advanced conversation. Andrey Andreyevitch, a good-natured bourgeois, suddenly declares: "Do you know, gentlemen, I was once an anarchist!" Every one is astonished. A. A. tells the following tale: a strict father; a technical school opened in the provincial town in a craze for technical education; they have no ideas and they did not know what to teach (since, if you are going to make shoemakers of all the inhabitants, who will buy the shoes?); he was expelled and his father turned him out of the house; he had to take a job as an assistant clerk on the squire's estate; he became enraged with the rich, the well-fed, and the fat; the squire planted cherry trees, A. A. helped him, and suddenly a desire came over him to cut off the squire's white fat fingers with the spade, as it if were by accident; and closing his eyes he struck a blow with the shovel as hard as he could, but it missed. Then he went away; the forest, the quiet in the fields, rain; he longed for warmth, went to his aunt, she gave him tea and rolls — and his anarchism was gone. After the story there passed by the table Councillor of State L. Immediately A. A. gets up and explains how L., Councillor of State, owns houses, etc.

I was apprenticed to a tailor. He cut the trousers; I did the sewing, but the stripe came down here right over the knee. Then I was apprenticed to a cabinet-maker. I was planing once when the plane flew out of my hands and hit the window; it broke the glass. The squire was a Lett, his name Shtoppev[1]; and he had an expression on his face as if he were going to wink and say: "Wouldn't it be nice to have a drink?" In the evenings he drank, drank by himself — and I felt hurt.

A dealer in cider puts labels on his bottles with a crown printed on them. It irritates and vexes X. who torments himself with the idea that a mere trader is usurping the crown. X. complains to the authorities, worries every

---

1 *Shtopov* means "cork-screw."

one, seeks redress and so on; he dies from irritation and worry.

A governess is teased with the nickname Gesticulation.

Shaptcherigin, Zambisebulsky, Sveentchutka, Chemburaklya.

Senile pomposity, senile vindictiveness. What a number of despicable old men I have known!

How delightful when on a bright frosty morning a new sleigh with a rug comes to the door.

X. arrived to take up duty at N., he shows himself a despot: he is annoyed when some one else is a success; he becomes quite different in the presence of a third person; when a woman is present, his tone changes; when he pours out wine, he first puts a little in his own glass and then helps the company; when he walks with a lady he takes her arm; in general he tries to show refinement. He does not laugh at other people's jokes: "You repeat yourself." "There is nothing new in that." Every one is sick of him; he sermonizes. The old women nickname him "the top."

A man who can not do anything, does not know how to act, how to enter a room, how to ask for anything.

Utiujny.

A man who always insists: "I haven't got syphilis. I'm an honest man. My wife is an honest woman."

X. all his life spoke and wrote about the vices of servants and about the way to manage and control them, and he died deserted by every one except his valet and his cook.

A little girl with rapture about her aunt: "She is very beautiful, as beautiful as our dog!"

Marie Ivạnovna Kolstovkin.

In a love letter: "Stamp enclosed for a reply."

The best men leave the villages for the towns, and therefore the villages decline and will continue to decline.

Pavel was a cook for forty years; he loathed the things which he cooked and he never ate.

He ceased to love a woman; the sensation of not being in love; a peaceful state of mind; long peaceful thoughts.

Conservative people do so little harm because they are timid and have no confidence in themselves; harm is done not by conservative but by malicious people.

One of two things: either sit in the carriage or get out of it.

For a play: an old woman of radical views dresses like a girl, smokes, cannot exist without company, sympathetic.

In a Pullman car — these are the dregs of society.

On the lady's bosom was the portrait of a fat German.

A man who at all elections all his life long always voted against the Left.

They undressed the corpse, but had no time to take the gloves off; a corpse in gloves.

A farmer at dinner boasts: "Life in the country is cheap — one has one's own chickens, one's own pigs — life is cheap."

A customs official, from want of love for his work, searches the passengers, looking for documents of a suspicious political nature, and makes even the gendarmes indignant.

A real male (mouzhtchina) consists of man (mouzh) and title (tchin).

Education: "Masticate your food properly," their father told them. And they masticated properly, and walked two hours every day, and washed in cold water, and yet they turned out unhappy and without talent.

Commercial and industrial medicine.

N. forty years old married a girl seventeen. The first night, when they returned to his mining village, she went to bed and suddenly burst into tears, because she did not love him.   He is a good soul, is overwhelmed with distress, and goes off to sleep in his little working room.

On the spot where the former manor house stood there is no trace left; only one lilac bush remains and that for some reason does not bloom.

Son: "To-day I believe is Thursday."
Mother: (not having heard) "What?"
Son: (angrily) "Thursday!" (quietly) "I ought to take a bath."
Mother: "What?"
Son: (angry and offended) "Bath!"

N. goes to X. every day, talks to him, and shows real sympathy in his grief; suddenly X. leaves his house, where he was so comfortable.   N. asks X.'s mother why he went away.   She answers: "Because you came to see him every day."

It was such a romantic wedding, and later — what fools! what babies!

Love.   Either it is a remnant of something degenerating, something which once has been immense, or it is a particle of what will in the future develop into something immense; but in the present it is unsatisfying, it gives much less than one expects.

A very intellectual man all his life tells lies about hypnotism, spiritualism — and people believe him; yet he is quite a nice man.

In Act I, X., a respectable man, borrows a hundred roubles from N., and in the course of all four acts he does not pay it back.

A grandmother has six sons and three daughters, and best of all she loves the failure, who drinks and has been in prison.

N., the manager of a factory, rich, with a wife and children, happy, has written "An investigation into the mineral spring at X." He was much praised for it and was invited to join the staff of a newspaper; he gave up his post, went to Petersburg, divorced his wife, spent his money — and went to the dogs.

(Looking at a photograph album): "Whose ugly face is that?"
"That's my uncle."

Alas, what is terrible is not the skeletons, but the fact that I am no longer terrified by them.

A boy of good family, capricious, full of mischief, obstinate, wore out his whole family. The father, an official who played the piano, got to hate him, took him into a corner of the garden, flogged him with considerable pleasure, and then felt disgusted with himself. The son has grown up and is an officer.

N. courted Z. for a long time. She was very religious, and, when he proposed to her, she put a dried flower, which he had once given to her, into her prayer-book.

Z: "As you are going to town, post my letter in the letter-box."

N: (alarmed) "Where? I don't know where the letter-box is."

Z: "Will you also call at the chemist's and get me some naphthaline?"

N: (alarmed) "I'll forget the naphthaline, I'll forget."

A storm at sea. Lawyers ought to regard it as a crime.

X. went to stay with his friend in the country. The place was magnificent, but the servants treated him badly, he was uncomfortable, although his friend considered him a big man. The bed was hard, he was not provided with a night shirt and he felt ashamed to ask for one.

At a rehearsal. The wife:
"How does that melody in Pagliacci go? Whistle it."
"One must not whistle on the stage; the stage is a temple."

He died from fear of cholera.

As like as a nail is to a requiem.

A conversation on another planet about the earth a thousand years hence. "Do you remember that white tree?"

Anakhthema!

Zigzagovsky, Oslizin, Svintchulka, Derbaliguin.

A woman with money, the money hidden everywhere, in her bosom and between her legs. . . .

All that procedure.

Treat your dismissal as you would an atmospheric phenomenon.

A conversation at a conference of doctors. First doctor: "All diseases can be cured by salt." Second doctor, military: "Every disease can be cured by prescribing no salt." The first points to his wife, the second to his daughter.

The mother has ideals, the father too; they delivered lectures; they built schools, museums, etc. They grow rich. And their children are most ordinary; spend money, gamble on the Stock Exchange.

N. married a German when she was seventeen. He took her to live in Berlin. At forty she became a widow and by that time spoke Russian badly and German badly.

The husband and wife loved having visitors, because, when there were no visitors they quarreled.

It is an absurdity! It is an anachronism!

"Shut the window! You are perspiring! Put on an overcoat! Put on galoshes!"

If you wish to have little spare time, do nothing.

On a Sunday morning in summer is heard the rumble of a carriage — people driving to mass.

For the first time in her life a man kissed her hand; it was too much for her, it turned her head.

What wonderful names: the little tears of Our Lady, warbler, crows-eyes.[1]

A government forest officer with shoulder straps, who has never seen a forest.

A gentleman owns a villa near Mentone; he bought it out of the proceeds of the sale of his estate in the Tula province. I saw him in Kharkhov to which he had come on business; he gambled away the villa at cards and became a railway clerk; after that he died.

At supper he noticed a pretty woman and choked; a little later he caught sight of another pretty woman and choked again, so that he did not eat his supper — there were a lot of pretty women.

A doctor, recently qualified, supervises the food in a restaurant. "The food is under the special supervision of a doctor." He copies out the chemical composition of the mineral water; the students believe him — and all is well.

He did not eat, he partook of food.

------

1 The names of flowers.

A man married to an actress during a performance of a play in which his wife was acting, sat in a box, with beaming face, and from time to time got up and bowed to the audience.

Dinner at Count O. D.'s. Fat lazy footmen; tasteless cutlets; a feeling that a lot of money is being spent, that the situation is hopeless, and that it is impossible to change the course of things.

A district doctor: "What other damned creature but a doctor would have to go out in such weather?" — he is proud of it, grumbles about it to every one, and is proud to think that his work is so troublesome; he does not drink and often sends articles to medical journals that do not publish them.

When N. married her husband, he was junior Public Prosecutor; he became judge of the High Court and then judge of the Court of Appeals; he is an average uninteresting man. N. loves her husband very much. She loves him to the grave, writes him meek and touching letters when she hears of his unfaithfulness, and dies with a touching expression of love on her lips. Evidently she loved, not her husband, but some one else, superior, beautiful, non-existent, and she lavished that love upon her husband. And after her death footsteps could be heard in her house.

They are members of a temperance society and now and again take a glass of wine.

They say: "In the long run truth will triumph;" but it is untrue.

A clever man says: "This is a lie, but since the people can not do without the lie, since it has the sanction of history, it is dangerous to root it out all at once; let it go on for the time being but with certain corrections." But the genius says: "This is a lie, therefore it must not exist."

Marie Ivanovna Kladovaya.

A schoolboy with mustaches, in order to show off, limps with one leg.

A writer of no talent, who has been writing for a long time, with his air of importance reminds one of a high priest.

Mr. N. and Miss Z. in the city of X. Both clever, educated, of radical views, and both working for the good of their fellow men, but both hardly know each other and in conversation always rail at each other in order to please the stupid and coarse crowd.

He flourished his hand as if he were going to seize him by the hair and said: "You won't escape by that there trick."

N. has never been in the country and thinks that in the winter country people use skis. "How I would enjoy ski-ing now!"

Madam N., who sells herself, says to each man who has her: "I love you because you are not like the rest."

An intellectual woman, or rather a woman who belongs to an intellectual circle, excels in deceit.

N. struggled all his life investigating a disease and studying its bacilli; he devoted his whole life to the struggle, expended on it all his powers, and suddenly just before his death it turned out that the disease is not in the least infectious or dangerous.

A theatrical manager, lying in bed, read a new play. He read three or four pages and then in irritation threw the play on to the floor, put out the candle, and drew the bed-clothes over him; a little later, after thinking over it, he took the play up again and began to read it; then, getting angry with the uninspired tedious work, he again threw it on the floor and put out the candle. A little later he once more took up the play and read it, then he produced it and it was a failure.

N., heavy, morose, gloomy, says: "I love a joke, I am always joking."

The wife writes; the husband does not like her writing, but out of delicacy says nothing and suffers all his life.

The fate of an actress: the beginning — a well-to-do family in Kerch, life dull and empty; the stage, virtue, passionate love, then lovers; the end: unsuccessful attempt to poison herself, then Kerch, life at her fat uncle's house, the delight of being left alone.   Experience shows that an artist must dispense with wine, marriage, pregnancy. The stage will become art only in the future, now it is only struggling for the future.

(Angrily and sententiously) "Why don't you give me your wife's letters to read?   Aren't we relations?"

Lord, don't allow me to condemn or to speak of what I do not know or do not understand.

Why do people describe only the weak, surly and frail as sinners?   And every one when he advises others to describe only the strong, healthy, and interesting, means himself.

For a play: a character always lying without rhyme or reason.

Sexton Catacombov.

N. N., a litterateur, critic, plausible, self-confident, very liberal minded, talks about poetry; condescendingly agrees with one — and I see that he is a man absolutely without talent (I haven't read him).   Some one suggests going to Ai-Petri.   I say that it is going to rain, but we set out. The road is muddy, it rains; the critic sits next to me, I feel his lack of talent.   He is wooed and made a fuss of as if he were a bishop.   And when it cleared up, I went back on foot. How easily people deceive themselves, how they love prophets and soothsayers; what a herd it is! Another person went with us, a Councillor of State, middle-aged, silent because he thinks he is right and despises the critic, because he too is without talent. A girl afraid to smile because she is among clever people.

Alexey Ivanitch Prokhladitelny (refreshing) or Doush-espasitelny (soul-saving). A girl: "I would marry him, but am afraid of the name — Madam Refreshing."

A dream of a keeper in the zoölogical gardens. He dreams that there was presented to the Zoo first a marmot, then an emu, then a vulture, then a she-goat, then another emu; the presentations are made without end and the Zoo is crowded out — the keeper wakes up in horror wet with perspiration.

"To harness slowly but drive rapidly is in the nature of this people," said Bismarck.

When an actor has money, he doesn't send letters but telegrams.

With insects, out of the caterpillar comes the butterfly; with mankind it is the other way round, out of the butterfly comes the caterpillar.[1]

The dogs in the house became attached not to their masters who fed and fondled them, but to the cook, a foreigner, who beat them.

---

[1] There is a play on words here, the Russian word for butterfly also means a woman.

Sophie was afraid that her dog might catch cold, because of the draught.

The soil is so good, that, were you to plant a shaft, in a year's time a cart would grow out of it.

X. and Z., very well educated and of radical views, married. In the evening they talked together pleasantly, then quarreled, then came to blows. In the morning both are ashamed and surprised, they think that it must have been the result of some exceptional state of their nerves. Next night again a quarrel and blows. And so every night until at last they realize that they are not at all educated, but savage, just like the majority of people.

A play: in order to avoid having visitors, Z. pretends to be a regular tippler although he drinks nothing.

When children appear on the scene then we justify all our weaknesses, our compromises, and our snobbery, by saying: "It's for the children's sake."

Count, I am going away to Mordegundia. (A land of horrible faces.)
Barbara Nedotypopin.

Z., an engineer or doctor, went on a visit to his uncle, an editor, he became interested, began to go there frequently; then became a contributor to the paper, little by little gave up his profession; one night he came out of the newspaper office, remembered, and seized his head in

his hands — "all is lost!" He began to go gray. Then it
became a habit, he was quite white now and flabby, an
editor, respectable but obscure.

A Privy Councillor, an old man, looking at his children,
became a radical himself.

A newspaper: "Cracknel."

The clown in the circus — that is talent, and the
waiter in the frock coat speaking to him — that is the
crowd; the waiter with an ironical smile on his face.

Auntie from Novozybkov.

He has a rarefaction of the brain and his brains have
leaked into his ears.

"What? Writers? If you like, for a shilling I'll make
a writer of you."

Instead of translator, contractor.

An actress, forty years old, ugly, ate a partridge for
dinner, and I felt sorry for the partridge, for it occurred
to me that in its life it had been more talented, more sensible, and more honest than that actress.

The doctor said to me: "If," says he, "your constitution holds out, drink to your heart's content." (Gorbunov.)

Carl Kremertartarlau.

A field with a distant view, one tiny birch tree. The inscription under the picture: loneliness.

The guests had gone: they had played cards and everything was in disorder: tobacco smoke, scraps of paper, and chiefly — the dawn and memories.

Better to perish from fools than to accept praises from them.

Why do trees grow and so luxuriantly, when the owners are dead?

The character keeps a library, but he is always away visiting; there are no readers.

Life seems great, enormous, and yet one sits on one's *piatachok.*[1]

Zolotonosha?[2] There is no such town! No!

When he laughs, he shows his teeth and gums.

He loved the sort of literature which did not upset him, Schiller, Homer, etc.

N., a teacher, on her way home in the evening was told by her friend that X. had fallen in love with her, N., and wanted to propose. N., ungainly, who had never before thought of marriage, when she got home, sat for a long

---

1 The word means five kopecks and also a pig's snout.
2 The name of a Russian town, meaning literally "Gold-carrier."

time trembling with fear, could not sleep, cried, and towards morning fell in love with X.; next day she heard that the whole thing was a supposition on the part of her friend and that X. was going to marry not her but Y.

He had a liaison with a woman of forty-five after which he began to write ghost stories.

I dreamt that I was in India and that one of the local princes presented me with an elephant, two elephants even. I was so worried about the elephant that I woke up.

An old man of eighty says to another old man of sixty: "You ought to be ashamed, young man."

When they sang in church, "Now is the beginning of our salvation," he ate *glavizna* at home; on the day of St. John the Baptist he ate no food that was circular and flogged his children.[1]

A journalist wrote lies in the newspaper, but he thought he was writing the truth.

If you are afraid of loneliness, do not marry.

He himself is rich, but his mother is in the workhouse.

He married, furnished a house, bought a writing-table, got everything in order, but found he had nothing to write.

---

1 *Glavizna* in Russian is the name of a fish and also means beginning; the root of the verbs "to behead" and "to flog" are the same.

Faust: "What you don't know is just what you want; what you know is what you can't use."

Although you may tell lies, people will believe you, if only you speak with authority.

As I shall lie in the grave alone, so in fact I live alone.

A German: "Lord have mercy on us, *grieshniki*." [1]

"O my dear little pimple!" said the bride tenderly. The bridegroom thought for a while, then felt hurt — they parted.

They were mineral water bottles with preserved cherries in them.

An actress who spoilt all her parts by very bad acting — and this continued all her life long until she died. Nobody liked her; she ruined all the best parts; and yet she went on acting until she was seventy.

He alone is all right and can repent who feels himself to be wrong.

The archdeacon curses the "doubters," and they stand in the choir and sing anathema to themselves (Skitalez).

He imagined that his wife lay with her legs cut off and that he nursed her in order to save his soul. . . .

---

1 *Grieshniki* means "sinners," but sounds like *grietchnieviki* which means "buckwheat cakes."

Madame Snuffley.

The black-beetles have left the house; the house will be burnt down.

"Dmitri, the Pretender, and Actors." "Turgenev and the Tigers." Articles like that can be and are written.

A title: Lemon Peel.

I am your legitimate husband.

An abortion, because while bathing a wave struck her, a wave of the ocean; because of the eruption of Vesuvius.

It seems to me: the sea and myself — and nothing else.

Education: his three-year-old son wore a black frock-coat, boots, and waistcoat.

With pride: "I'm not of Yuriev, but of Dorpat University." [1]

His beard looked like the tail of a fish.

A Jew, Ziptchik.

A girl, when she giggles, makes noises as if she were putting her head in cold water.

"Mamma, what is a thunderbolt made of?"

---

1 Yuriev is the Russian name of the town Dorpat.

On the estate there is a bad smell, and bad taste; the trees are planted anyhow, stupidly; and away in a remote corner the lodge-keeper's wife all day long washes the guest's linen — and nobody sees her; and the owners are allowed to talk away whole days about their rights and their nobility.

She fed her dog on the best caviare.

Our self-esteem and conceit are European, but our culture and actions are Asiatic.

A black dog — he looks as if he were wearing galoshes.

A Russian's only hope — to win two hundred thousand roubles in a lottery.

She is wicked but she taught her children good.

Every one has something to hide.

The title of N.'s story: The Power of Harmonies.

O how nice it would be if bachelors or widowers were appointed Governors.

A Moscow actress never in her life saw a turkey-hen.

On the lips of the old I hear either stupidity or malice.

"Mamma, Pete did not say his prayers." Pete is woken up, he says his prayers, cries, then lies down and shakes his fist at the child who made the complaint.

He imagined that only doctors could say whether it is male or female.

One became a priest, the other a *Dukhobor*, the third a philosopher, and in each case instinctively because no one wants really to work with bent back from morning to night.

A passion for the word uterine: my uterine brother, my uterine wife, my uterine brother-in-law, etc.

To Doctor N., an illegitimate child, who has never lived with his father and knew him very little, his bosom friend Z., says with agitation: "You see, the fact of the matter is that your father misses you very much, he is ill and wants to have a look at you." The father keeps "Switzerland," furnished apartments. He takes the fried fish out of the dish with his hands and only afterwards uses a fork. The vodka smells rank. N. went, looked about him, had dinner — his only feeling that that fat peasant, with the grizzled beard, should sell such filth. But once, when passing the house at midnight, he looked in at the window: his father was sitting with bent back reading a book. He recognized himself and his own manners.

As stupid as a gray gelding.

They teased the girl with castor oil, and therefore she did not marry.

N. all his life used to write abusive letters to famous singers, actors, and authors: "You think, you scamp, . . ." — without signing his name.

When the man who carried the torch at funerals came out in his three-cornered hat, his frock coat with laces and stripes, she fell in love with him.

A sparkling, joyous nature, a kind of living protest against grumblers; he is fat and healthy, eats a great deal, every one likes him but only because they are afraid of the grumblers; he is a nobody, a Ham, only eats and laughs loud, and that's all; when he dies, every one sees that he had done nothing, that they had mistaken him for some one else.

After the inspection of the building, the Commission, which was bribed, lunched heartily, and it was precisely a funeral feast over honesty.

He who tells lies is dirty.

At three o'clock in the morning they wake him: he has to go to his job at the railway station, and so every day for the last fourteen years.

A lady grumbles: "I write to my son that he should change his linen every Saturday." He replies: 'Why Saturday, not Monday?' I answer: "Well, all right, let it be Monday." And he: 'Why Monday, not Tuesday?' He is a nice honest man, but I get worried by him."

A clever man loves learning but is a fool at teaching.

The sermons of priests, archimandrites, and bishops are wonderfully like one another.

One remembers the arguments about the brotherhood of man, public good, and work for the people, but really there were no such arguments, one only drank at the University. They write: "One feels ashamed of the men with University degrees who once fought for human rights and freedom of religion and conscience" — but they never fought.

Every day after dinner the husband threatens his wife that he will become a monk, and the wife cries.

Mordokhvostov.

Husband and wife have lived together and quarreled for eighteen years. At last he makes a confession, which was in fact untrue, of having been false to her, and they part to his great pleasure and to the wrath of the whole town.

A useless thing, an album with forgotten, uninteresting photographs, lies in the corner on a chair; it has been lying there for the last twenty years and one makes up his mind to throw it away.

N. tells how forty years ago X., a wonderful and extra-ordinary man, had saved the lives of five people, and N.

feels it strange that every one listened with indifference, that the history of X. is already forgotten, uninteresting. . . .

They fell upon the soft caviare greedily, and devoured it in a minute.

In the middle of a serious conversation he says to his little son: "Button up your trousers."

Man will only become better when you make him see what he is like.

Dove-colored face.

The squire feeds his pigeons, canaries, and fowls on pepper, acids, and all kinds of rubbish in order that the birds may change their color — and that is his sole occupation: he boasts of it to every visitor.

They invited a famous singer to recite the Acts of the Apostles at the wedding; he recited it, but they have not paid his fee.

For a farce: I have a friend by name Krivomordy (crooked face) and he's all right. Not crooked leg or crooked arm but crooked face: he was married and his wife loved him.

N. drank milk every day, and every time he put a fly in the glass and then, with the air of a victim, asked the old butler: "What's that?" He could not live a single day without that.

She is surly and smells of a vapor bath.

N. learned of his wife's adultery. He is indignant, distressed, but hesitates and keeps silent. He keeps silence and ends by borrowing money from Z., the lover, and continues to consider himself an honest man.

When I stop drinking tea and eating bread and butter, I say: "I have had enough." But when I stop reading poems or novels, I say: "No more of that, no more of that."

A solicitor lends money at a high rate of interest, and justifies himself because he is leaving everything to the University of Moscow.

A little sexton, with radical views: "Nowadays our fellows crawl out from all sorts of unexpected holes."

The squire N. always quarrels with his neighbors who are Molokans [1]; he goes to court, abuses and curses them; but when at last they leave, he feels there is an empty place; he ages rapidly and pines away.

Mordukhanov.

With N. and his wife there lives the wife's brother, a lachrymose young man who at one time steals, at another

---

1 Molokans are a religious sect in Russia.

tells lies, at another attempts suicide; N. and his wife do not know what to do, they are afraid to turn him out because he might kill himself; they would like to turn him out, but they do not know how to manage it. For forging a bill he gets into prison, and N. and his wife feel that they are to blame; they cry, grieve. She died from grief; he too died some time later and everything was left to the brother who squandered it and got into prison again.

Suppose I had to marry a woman and live in her house, I would run away in two days, but a woman gets used so quickly to her husband's house, as though she had been born there.

Well, you are a Councillor; but whom do you counsel? God forbid that any one should listen to your counsels.

The little town of Torjok. A sitting of the town council. Subject: the raising of the rates. Decision: to invite the Pope to settle down in Torjok — to choose it as his residence.

S.'s logic: I am for religious toleration, but against religious freedom; one cannot allow what is not in the strict sense orthodox.

St. Piony and Epinach. ii March, Pupli 13 m.

Poetry and works of art contain not what is needed but what people desire; they do not go further than the crowd and they express only what the best in the crowd desire.

A little man is very cautious; he sends even letters of congratulation by registered post in order to get a receipt.

Russia is an enormous plain across which wander mischievous men.

Platonida Ivanovna.

If you are politically sound, that is enough for you to be considered a perfectly satisfactory citizen; the same thing with radicals, to be politically unsound is enough, everything else will be ignored.

A man who when he fails opens his eyes wide.

Ziuzikov.

A Councillor of State, a respectable man; it suddenly comes out that he has secretly kept a brothel.

N. has written a good play; no one praises him or is pleased; they all say: "We'll see what you write next."

The more important people came in by the front door, the simple folk by the back door.

He: "And in our town there lived a man whose name was Kishmísh (raisin). He called himself Kíshmish, but every one knew that he was Kishmísh."
She (after some thought): "How annoying . . . if only his name had been Sultana, but Kíshmish! . . ."

Blagovospitanny.

Most honored Iv-Iv-itch!

How intolerable people are sometimes who are happy and successful in everything.   .

They begin gossiping that N. is living with Z.; little by little an atmosphere is created in which a liaison of N. and Z. becomes inevitable.

When the locust was a plague, I wrote against the locust and enchanted every one, I was rich and famous; but now, when the locust has long ago disappeared and is forgotten, I am merged in the crowd, forgotten, and not wanted.

Merrily, joyfully: "I have the honor to introduce you to Iv. Iv. Izgoyev, my wife's lover."

Everywhere on the estate are notices: "Trespassers will be prosecuted," "Keep off the flowers," etc.

In the great house is a fine library which is talked about but is never used; they give you watery coffee which you cannot drink; the garden is tasteless with no flowers in it — and they pretend that all this is something Tolstoyan.

He learnt Swedish in order to study Ibsen, spent a lot of time and trouble, and suddenly realized that Ibsen is not important; he could not conceive what use he could now make of the Swedish language.[1]

N. makes a living by exterminating bugs; and for the purposes of his trade he reads the works of——. If in "The Cossacks," bugs are not mentioned, it means that "The Cossacks" is a bad book.

Man is what he believes.

A clever girl: "I cannot pretend . . . I never tell a lie . . . I have principles" — and all the time "I . . . I . . . I . . ."

N. is angry with his wife who is an actress, and without her knowledge gets abusive criticisms published about her in the newspapers.

A nobleman boasts "This house of mine was built in the time of Dmitry Donskoy."

"Your Worship, he called my dog a bad name: 'son of a bitch.' "

---

1 Ibsen wrote in Norwegian of course. Responding to a request for his interpretation of this curious paragraph. Mr. Koteliansky writes:

"Chekhov had a very high opinion of Ibsen; the paragraph, I am sure, is by no means aimed at Ibsen. Most probably the paragraph, as well as many others in the Notes, is something which C. either personally or indirectly heard someone say. You will see that Kuprin ["Reminiscences of Chekhov," by Gorky, Kuprin and Bunin, New York: Huebsch.] told C. the anecdote about the actor whose wife asked him to whistle a melody on the stage during a rehearsal. In C.'s Notes you have that anecdote, somewhat shortened and the names changed, without mentioning the source.

"The reader, on the whole, may puzzle his head over many paragraphs in the Notes, but he will hardly find explanations each time. What the reader has to remember is that the Notes are material used by C. in his creative activity and as such it throws a great deal of light on C.'s mentality and process of working."

The snow fell and did not lie on the ground reddened with blood.

He left everything to charity, so that nothing should go to his relations and children, whom he hated.

A very amorous man; he is no sooner introduced to a girl than he becomes a he-goat.

A nobleman Drekoliev.

I dread the idea that a chamberlain will be present at the opening of my petition.

He was a rationalist, but he had to confess he liked the ringing of church bells.

The father a famous general, nice pictures, expensive furniture; he died; the daughters received a good education, but are slovenly, read little, ride, and are dull.

They are honest and truthful so long as it is unnecessary.

A rich merchant would like to have a shower bath in his W. C.

In the early morning they ate *okroshka*. [1]

"If you lose this talisman," said grandmother, "you will die." And suddenly I lost it, tortured myself, was afraid

_____

1 A cold dish composed of cider and hash.

that I would die. And now, imagine, a miracle happened: I found it and continued to live.

Everybody goes to the theatre to see my play, to learn something instantly from it, to make some sort of profit, and I tell you: I have not the time to bother about that canaille.

The people hate and despise everything new and useful; when there was cholera, they hated and killed the doctors and they love vodka; by the people's love or hatred one can estimate the value of what they love or hate.

Looking out of the window at the corpse which is being borne to the cemetery: "You are dead, you are being carried to the cemetery, and I will go and have my breakfast."

A Tchech Vtitchka.

A man, forty years old, married a girl of twenty-two who read only the very latest writers, wore green ribbons, slept on yellow pillows, and believed in her taste and her opinions as if they were law; she is nice, not silly, and gentle, but he separates from her.

When one longs for a drink, it seems as though one could drink a whole ocean — that is faith; but when one begins to drink, one can only drink altogether two glasses — that is science.

For a farce: Fildekosov, Poprygunov.

In former times a nice man, with principles, who wanted to be respected, would try to become a general or priest, but now he goes in for being a writer, professor. . . .

There is nothing which history will not justify.

Zievoulia. [1]

The crying of a nice child is ugly; so in bad verses you may recognize that the author is a nice man.

If you wish women to love you, be original; I know a man who used to wear felt boots summer and winter, and women fell in love with him.

I arrive at Yalta. Every room is engaged. I go to the "Italy" — not a room available. "What about my room number 35" — "It is engaged." A lady. They say: "Would you like to stay with this lady? The lady has no objection." I stay in her room. Conversation. Evening. The Tartar guide comes in. My ears are stopped, my eyes blindfolded; I sit and see nothing and hear nothing. . . .

A young lady complains: "My poor brother gets such a small salary — only seven thousand!"

She: "I see only one thing now: you have a large mouth! A large mouth! An enormous mouth!"

---

1 A name or word invented by Chekhov meaning "One who yawns for a long time with pleasure."

The horse is a useless and pernicious animal; a great deal of land has to be tilled for it, it accustoms man not to employ his own muscles, it is often an object of luxury; it makes man effeminate. For the future not a single horse.

N. a singer; speaks to nobody, his throat muffled up — he takes care of his voice, but no one has ever heard him sing.

About absolutely everything: "What's the good of that? It's useless!"

He wears felt boots summer and winter and gives this explanation: "It's better for the head, because the blood, owing to the heat, is drawn down into the feet, and the thoughts are clearer."

A woman is jocularly called Fiodor Ivanovitch.

A farce: N., in order to marry, greased the bald patch on his head with an ointment which he read of in an advertisement, and suddenly there began to grow on his head pig's bristles.

What does your husband do? — He takes castor oil.

A girl writes: "We shall live intolerably near you."

N. has been for long in love with Z. who married X.; two years after the marriage Z. comes to N., cries, wishes to tell him something; N. expects to hear her complain against her husband; but it turns out that Z. has come to tell of her love for K.

N. a well known lawyer in Moscow; Z., who like N. was born in Taganrog, comes to Moscow and goes to see the celebrity; he is received warmly, but he remembers the school to which they both went, remembers how N. looked in his uniform, becomes agitated by envy, sees that N.'s flat is in bad taste, that N. himself talks a great deal; and he leaves disenchanted by envy and by the meanness which before he did not even suspect was in him.

The title of a play: The Bat.

Everything which the old cannot enjoy is forbidden or considered wrong.

When he was getting on in years, he married a very young girl, and so she faded and withered away with him.

All his life he wrote about capitalism and millions, and he had never had any money.

A young lady fell in love with a handsome constable.

N. was a very good, fashionable tailor; but he was spoiled and ruined by trifles; at one time he made an overcoat without pockets, at another a collar which was much too high.

A farce: Agent or freight transport company and of fire insurance company.

Any one can write a play which might be produced.

A country house. Winter. N., ill, sits in his room. In the evening there suddenly arrives from the railway station a stranger Z., a young girl, who introduces herself and says that she has come to look after the invalid. He is perplexed, frightened, he refuses; then Z. says that at any rate she will stay the night. A day passes, two, and she goes on living there. She has an unbearable temper, she poisons one's existence.

A private room in a restaurant. A rich man Z., tying his napkin round his neck, touching the sturgeon with his fork: "At least I'll have a snack before I die" — and he has been saying this for a long time, daily.

By his remarks on Strindberg and literature generally L. L. Tolstoy reminds one very much of Madam Loukhmav. [1]

Diedlov, when he speaks of the Deputy Governor or the Governor, becomes a romanticist, remembering "The Arrival of the Deputy Governor" in the book *A Hundred Russian Writers*.

A play: the Bean of Life.

A vet. belongs to the stallion class of people.

Consultation.

----

1 L. L. Tolstoy was Leo Nicolaievitch's son, Madame Loukhmav a tenth rate woman writer.

The sun shines and in my soul is darkness.

In S. I made the acquaintance of the barrister Z. — a sort of Nika, The Fair. . . . He has several children; with all of them he is magisterial, gentle, kind, not a single rude word; I soon learn that he has another family. Then he invites me to his daughter's wedding; he prays, makes a genuflection, and says: "I still preserve religious feeling; I am a believer." And when in his presence people speak of education, of women, he has a naïve expression, exactly as if he did not understand. When he makes a speech in Court, his face looks as if he were praying.

"Mammy, don't show yourself to the guests, you are very fat."

Love? In Love? Never! I am a Government clerk.

He knows little, even as a babe who has not yet come out of his mother's womb.

From childhood until extreme old age N. has had a passion for spying.

He uses clever words, that's all — philosophy . . . equator . . . (for a play).

The stars have gone out long ago, but they still shine for the crowd.

As soon as he became a scholar, he began to expect honors.

He was a prompter, but got disgusted and gave it up; for about fifteen years he did not go to the theatre; then he went and saw a play, cried with emotion, felt sad, and, when his wife asked him on his return how to liked the theatre, he answered: "I do not like it."

The parlormaid Nadya fell in love with an exterminator of bugs and black beetles.

A Councillor of State; it came out after his death that, in order to earn a rouble, he was employed at the theatre to bark like a dog; he was poor.

You must have decent, well-dressed children, and your children too must have a nice house and children, and their children again children and nice houses; and what is it all for? — The devil knows.

Perkaturin.

Every day he forces himself to vomit — for the sake of his health, on the advice of a friend.

A Government official began to live an original life; a very tall chimney on his house, green trousers, blue waist-coat, a dyed dog, dinner at midnight; after a week he gave it up.

Success has already given that man a lick with its tongue.

In the bill presented by the hotel-keeper was among other things: "Bugs — fifteen kopecks." Explanation.

"N. has fallen into poverty." — "What? I can't hear." — "I say N. has fallen into poverty." — "What exactly do you say? I can't make out. What N.?" — "The N. who married Z." — "Well, what of it?" — "I say we ought to help him." — "Eh? What him? Why help? What do you mean?" — and so on.

How pleasant to sit at home, when the rain is drumming on the roof, and to feel that there are no heavy dull guests coming to one's house.

N. always even after five glasses of wine, takes valerian drops.

He lives with a parlormaid who respectfully calls him Your Honor.

I rented a country house for the summer; the owner, a very fat old lady, lived in the lodge, I in the great house; her husband was dead and so were all her children, she was left alone, very fat, the estate sold for debt, her furniture old and in good taste; all day long she reads letters which her husband and son had written to her. Yet she is an optimist. When some one fell ill in my house, she smiled and said again and again: "My dear, God will help."

N. and Z. are school friends, each seventeen or eighteen

years old; and suddenly N. learns that Z. is with child by N.'s father.

The priezt came . . . zaint . . . praize to thee, O Lord.

What empty words these discussions about the rights of women! If a dog writes a work of talent, they will even accept the dog.

Hæmorrhage: "It's an abscess that's just burst inside you . . . it's all right, have some more vodka."

The intelligentsia are good for nothing, because they drink a lot of tea, talk a lot in stuffy rooms, with empty bottles.

When she was young, she ran away with a doctor, a Jew, and had a daughter by him; now she hates her past, hates the red-haired daughter, and the father still loves her as well as the daughter, and walks under her window, chubby and handsome.

He picked his teeth and put the toothpick back into the glass.

The husband and wife could not sleep; they began to discuss how bad literature had become and how nice it would be to publish a magazine: the idea carried them away; they lay awake silent for awhile. "Shall we ask Boborykin to write?" he asked. "Certainly, do ask him."

At five in the morning he starts for his work at the depot; she sees him off walking in the snow to the gate, shuts the gate after him. . . . "And shall we ask Potapenko?" he asks, already outside the gate.

When he learnt that his father had been raised to the nobility he began to sign himself Alexis.

Teacher: " 'The collision of a train with human victims' . . . that is wrong . . . it ought to be 'the collision of a train that resulted in human victims' . . . for the cause of the people on the line."

Title of play: Golden Rain.

There is not a single criterion which can serve as the measure of the non-existent, of the non-human.

A patriot: "And do you know that our Russian macaroni is better than the Italian? I'll prove it to you. Once at Nice they brought me sturgeon — do you know, I nearly cried." And the patriot did not see that he was only gastronomically patriotic.

A grumbler: "But is turkey food? Is caviare food?"

A very sensible, clever young woman; when she was bathing, he noticed that she had a narrow pelvis and pitifully thin hips — and he got to hate her.

A clock. Yegor the locksmith's clock at one time loses and at another gains exactly as if to spite him; deliberately

it is now at twelve and then quite suddenly at eight. It
does it out of animosity as though the devil were in it.
The locksmith tries to find out the cause, and once he
plunges it in holy water.

Formerly the heroes in novels and stories (e.g. Petchorin,
Onegin) were twenty years old, but now one cannot
have a hero under thirty to thirty-five years. The same
will soon happen with heroines.

N. is the son of a famous father; he is very nice, but,
whatever he does, every one says: "That is very well, but
it is nothing to the father." Once he gave a recitation at
an evening party; all the performers had a success, but of
him they said: "That is very well, but still it is nothing to
the father." He went home and got into bed, and, looking at his father's portrait, shook his fist at him.

We fret ourselves to reform life, in order that posterity
may be happy, and posterity will say as usual: "In the
past it used to be better, the present is worse than the past."

My motto: I don't want anything.

When a decent working-man takes himself and his
work critically, people call him grumbler, idler, bore; but
when an idle scoundrel shouts that it is necessary to work,
he is applauded.

When a woman destroys things like a man, people think
it natural and everybody understands it; but when like a

man, she wishes or tries to create, people think it un-natural and cannot reconcile themselves to it.

When I married, I became an old woman.

He looked down on the world from the height of his baseness.

"Your fiancée is very pretty." "To me all women are alike."

He dreamt of winning three hundred thousand in lottery, twice in succession, because three hundred thousand would not be enough for him.

N., a retired Councillor of State, lives in the country; he is sixty-six. He is educated, liberal-minded, reads, likes an argument. He learns from his guests that the new coroner Z. walks about with a slipper on one foot and a boot on the other, and lives with another man's wife. N. thinks all the time of Z.; he does nothing but talk about him, how he walks about in one slipper and lives with another man's wife; he talks of nothing else; at last he goes to sleep with his own wife (he has not slept with her for the last eight years), he is agitated and the whole time talks about Z. Finally he has a stroke, his arm and leg are paralyzed — and all this from agitation about Z. The doctor comes. With him too N. talks about Z. The doctor says that he knows Z., that Z. now wears two boots, his leg being well, and that he has married the lady.

I hope that in the next world I shall be able to look back at this life and say: "Those were beautiful dreams. . . ."

The squire N., looking at the undergraduate and the young girl, the children of his steward Z.: "I am sure Z. steals from me, lives grandly on stolen money, the undergraduate and the girl know it or ought to know it; why then do they look so decent?"

She is fond of the word "compromise," and often uses it; "I am incapable of compromise. . . ." "A board which has the shape of a parallelepiped."

The hereditary honorable citizen Oziaboushkin always tries to make out that his ancestors had the right to the title of Count.

"He is a perfect dab at it." "O, O, don't use that expression; my mother is very particular."

I have just married my third husband . . . the name of the first was Ivan Makarivitch . . . of the second Peter . . . Peter . . . I have forgotten."

The writer Gvozdikov thinks that he is very famous, that every one knows him. He arrives at S., meets an officer who shakes his hand for a long time, looking with rapture into his face. G. is glad, he too shakes hands warmly. . . . At last the officer: "And how is your orchestra? Aren't you the conductor?"

Morning; M.'s mustaches are in curl papers.

And it seemed to him that he was highly respected and valued everywhere, anywhere, even in railway buffets, and so he always ate with a smile on his face.

The birds sing, and already it begins to seem to him that they do not sing, but whine.

N., father of a family, listens to his son reading aloud J. J. Rousseau to the family, and thinks: "Well, at any rate, J. J. Rousseau had no gold medal on his breast, but I have one."

N. has a spree with his step-son, an undergraduate, and they go to a brothel. In the morning the undergraduate is going away, his leave is up; N. sees him off. The undergraduate reads him a sermon on their bad behavior; they quarrel. N.: "As your father, I curse you." — "And I curse you."

A doctor is called in, but a nurse sent for.

N. N. V. never agrees with anyone: "Yes, the ceiling is white, that can be admitted; but white, as far as is known, consists of the seven colors of the spectrum, and it is quite possible that in this case one of the colors is darker or brighter than is necessary for the production of pure white; I had rather think a bit before saying that the ceiling is white."

He holds himself exactly as though he were an icon.

"Are you in love?" — "There's a little bit of that in it."

Whatever happens, he says: "It is the priests."

Firzikov.

N. dreams that he is returning from abroad, and that at Verzhbolovo, in spite of his protests, they make him pay duty on his wife.

When that radical, having dined with his coat off, walked into his bedroom and I saw the braces on his back, it became clear to me that that radical is a bourgeois, a hopeless bourgeois.

Some one saw Z., an unbeliever and blasphemer, secretly praying in front of the icon in the cathedral, and they all teased him.

They called the manager "four-funneled cruiser," because he had already gone "through the chimney" (bankrupt) four times.

He is not stupid, he was at the university, has studied long and assiduously, but in writing he makes gross mistakes.

Countess Nadin's daughter gradually turns into a housekeeper; she is very timid, and can only say "No-o," "Yes-s," and her hands always tremble. Somehow or other a Zemstvo official wished to marry her; he is a widower and she marries him, with him too it was "Yes-s," "No-o"; she was very much afraid of her husband and did not love him; one day he happened to give a loud cough, it gave her a fright, and she died.

Caressing her lover: "My vulture."

For a play: If only you would say something funny. But for twenty years we have lived together and you have always talked of serious things; I hate serious things.

A cook, with a cigarette in her mouth, lies: "I studied at a high school . . . I know what for the earth is round."

"Society for finding and raising anchors of steamers and barges," and the Society's agent at all functions without fail makes a speech, à la N., and without fail promises.

Super-mysticism.

When I become rich, I shall have a harem in which I shall keep fat naked women, with their buttocks painted green.

A shy young man came on a visit for the night: suddenly a deaf old woman came into his room, carrying a cupping-glass, and bled him; he thought that this must be the usual thing and so did not protest; in the morning it turned out that the old woman had made a mistake.

Surname: Verstax.

The more stupid the peasant, the better does the horse understand him.

. . . How stupid and for the most part how false, since if one man seeks to devour another or tell him something unpleasant it has nothing to do with Granovsky. [1]

I left Gregory Ivanovitch's feeling crushed and mortally offended. I was irritated by smooth words and by those who speak them, and on reaching home I meditated thus: some rail at the world, others at the crowd, that is to say praise the past and blame the present; they cry out that there are no ideals and so on, but all this has already been said twenty or thirty years ago; these are worn-out forms which have already served their time, and whoever repeats them now, he too is no longer young and is himself worn out. With last year's foliage there decay too those who live in it. I thought, we uncultured, worn-out people, banal in speech, stereotyped in intentions, have grown quite mouldy, and, while we intellectuals are rummaging among old rags and, according to the old Russian custom, biting one another, there is boiling up around us a life which we neither know nor notice. Great events will take us unawares, like sleeping fairies, and you will see that Sidorov, the merchant, and the teacher of the school at Yeletz, who see and know more than we do, will push us far into the background, because they will accomplish more than all of us put together. And I thought that were we now to obtain political liberty, of which we talk so much, while engaged in biting one another, we should not know what to do with it, we should waste it in accus-

---

1 A well-known Radical professor, a Westerner.

ing one another in the newspapers of being spies and money-grubbers, we should frighten society with the assurance that we have neither men, nor science, nor literature, nothing! Nothing! And to scare society as we are doing now, and as we shall continue to do, means to deprive it of courage; it means simply to declare that we have no social or political sense in us. And I also thought that, before the dawn of a new life has broken, we shall turn into sinister old men and women and we shall be the first who, in our hatred of that dawn, will calumniate it.

Mother never stops talking about poverty. It is very strange. In the first place, it is strange that we are poor, beg like beggars, and at the same time eat superbly, live in a large house; in the summer we go to our own country house, and generally speaking we do not look like beggars. Evidently this is not poverty, but something else, and rather worse. Secondly, it is strange that for the last ten years mother has been spending all her energy solely on getting money to pay interest. It seems to me that were mother to spend that terrible energy on something else, we could have twenty such houses. Thirdly, it seems to me strange that the hardest work in the family is done by mother, not by me. To me that is the strangest thing of all, most terrible. She has, as she has just said, a thought on her brain, she begs, she humiliates herself; our debts grow daily and up till now I have not done a single thing to help her. What can I do? I think and think and cannot make it out. I only see clearly that we are rushing down an inclined plane, but to what, the devil knows. They say that poverty threatens us and that in poverty there is disgrace, but that too I cannot understand, since I was never poor.

The spiritual life of these women is as gray and dull as their faces and dresses; they speak of science, literature, tendencies, and the like, only because they are the wives and sisters of scholars and literary men; were they the wives and sisters of inspectors or of dentists, they would speak with the same zeal of fires or teeth. To allow them to speak of science, which is foreign to them, and to listen to them, is to flatter their ignorance.

Essentially all this is crude and meaningless, and romantic love appears as meaningless as an avalanche which involuntarily rolls down a mountain and overwhelms people. But when one listens to music, all this is: that some people lie in their graves and sleep, and that one woman is alive — gray-haired, she is sitting in a box in the theatre, quiet and majestic, and the avalanche seems no longer meaningless, since in nature everything has a meaning. And everything is forgiven, and it would be strange not to forgive.

Olga Ivanovna regarded old chairs, stools, sofas, with the same respectful tenderness as she regarded old dogs and horses, and her room, therefore, was something like an almshouse for furniture. Round the mirror, on all tables and shelves, stood photographs of uninteresting, half-forgotten people; on the walls hung pictures at which nobody ever looked; and it was always dark in the room, because there burnt there only one lamp with a blue shade.

If you cry "Forward," you must without fail explain in which direction one must go. Do you not see that, if without explaining the direction, you fire off this word simultaneously at a monk and at a revolutionary, they will proceed in precisely opposite directions?

It is said in Holy Writ: "Fathers, do not irritate your children," even the wicked and good-for-nothing children; but the fathers irritate me, irritate me terribly. My contemporaries chime in with them and the youngsters follow, and every minute they strike me in the face with their smooth words.

That the aunt suffered and did not show it gave him the impression of a trick.

O. I. was in constant motion; such women, like bees, carry about a fertilizing pollen. . . .

Don't marry a rich woman — she will drive you out of the house; don't marry a poor woman — you won't sleep; but marry the freest freedom, the lot and life of a Cossack. (Ukrainian saying.)

Aliosha: "I often hear people say: 'Before marriage there is romance, and then — goodbye, illusion!' How heartless and coarse it is."

So long as a man likes the splashing of a fish, he is a poet; but when he knows that the splashing is nothing but the chase of the weak by the strong, he is a thinker;

but when he does not understand what sense there is in the chase, or what use in the equilibrium which results from destruction, he is becoming silly and dull, as he was when a child. And the more he knows and thinks, the sillier he becomes.

The death of a child. I have no sooner sat down in peace than — bang — fate lets fly at me.

The she-wolf, nervous and anxious, fond of her young, dragged away a foal into her winter-shelter, thinking him a lamb. She knew that there was a ewe there and that the ewe had young. While she was dragging the foal away, suddenly some one whistled; she was alarmed and dropped him, but he followed her. They arrived at the shelter. He began to suck like the young wolves. Throughout the winter he changed but little; he only grew thin and his legs longer, and the spot on his forehead turned into a triangle. The she-wolf was in delicate health. [1]

They invited celebrities to these evening parties, and it was dull because there are few people of talent in Moscow, and the same singers and reciters performed at all evening parties.

She has not before felt herself so free and easy with a man.

----

[1] A sketch of part of the story "Whitehead."

You wait until you grow up and I'll teach you declamation.

It seemed to her that at the show many of the pictures were alike.

There filed up before you a whole line of laundry-maids.

Kostya insisted that the women had robbed themselves.

L. put himself in the place of the juryman and interpreted it thus: if it was a case of house-breaking, then there was no theft, because the laundresses themselves sold the linen and spent the money on drink; but if it was a case of theft, then there could have been no house-breaking.

Fiodor was flattered that his brother had found him at the same table with a famous actor.

When Y. spoke or ate, his beard moved as if he had no teeth in his mouth.

Ivashin loved Nadya Vishnyevsky and was afraid of his love. When the butler told him that the old lady has just gone out, but the young lady was at home, he fumbled in his fur coat and dress-coat pocket, found his card, and said: "Right."

But it was not all right. Driving from his house in the morning, to pay a visit, he thought that he was compelled to it by conventions of society, which weighed heavily upon him. But now it was clear to him that he went to pay calls only because somewhere far away in the depths of his soul, as under a veil, there lay hidden a hope that he would see Nadya. . . . And he suddenly felt pitiful, sad, and a little frightened. . . .

In his soul, it seemed to him, it was snowing, and everything faded away. He was afraid to love Nadya, because he was too old for her, thought his appearance unattractive, and did not believe that young girls like Nadya could love men for their minds and spiritual qualities. Still there would at times rise in him something like a hope. But now, from the moment when the officer's spurs jingled and then died away, there also died away his timid love. . . . All was at an end, hope was impossible. . . . "Yes, now all is finished," he thought, "I am glad, very glad."

He imagined his wife to be not Nadya, but always, for some reason, a stout woman with a large bosom, covered with Venetian lace.

The clerks in the office of the Governor of the island have a drunken headache. They long for a drink. They have no money. What is to be done? One of them, a convict who is serving his time here for forgery, devises a plan. He goes to the church, where a former officer, now exiled for giving his superior a box on the ears, sings in the choir, and says to him panting: "Here! There's a pardon come for you! They have got a telegram in the office."

The late officer turns pale, trembles, and can hardly walk for excitement.

"But for such news you ought to give something for a drink," says the clerk.

"Take all I have! All!"

And he hands him some five roubles. . . . He arrives at the office. The officer is afraid that he may die from joy and presses his hand to his heart.

"Where is the telegram?"

"The bookkeeper has put it away." (He goes to the bookkeeper.) General laughter and an invitation to drink with them.

"How terrible!"

After that the officer was ill for a week. [1]

Fedya, the steward's brother-in-law, told Ivanov that wild-duck were feeding on the other side of the wood. He loaded his gun with slugs. Suddenly a wolf appeared. He fired and smashed both the wolf's hips. The wolf was mad with pain and did not see him. "What can I do for you, dear?" He thought and thought, and then went home and called Peter. . . . Peter took a stick, and with an awful grimace, began to beat the wolf. . . . He beat and beat and beat until it died. . . . .He broke into a sweat and went away, without saying a single word.

Vera: "I do not respect you, because you married so strangely, because nothing came of you. . . . That is why I have secrets from you."

---

1 An episode which Chekhov heard during his journey in the island, Sakhalin.

It is unfortunate that we try to solve the simplest questions cleverly, and therefore make them unusually complicated. We should seek a simple solution.

There is no Monday which will not give its place to Tuesday.

I am happy and satisfied, sister, but if I were born a second time and were asked: "Do you want to marry?" I should answer: "No." "Do you want to have money?" "No. . . ."

Lenstchka liked dukes and counts in novels, not ordinary persons. She loved the chapters in which there is love, pure and ideal not sensual. Descriptions of nature she did not like. She preferred conversations to descriptions. While reading the beginning she would glance impatiently at the end. She did not remember the names of authors. She wrote with a pencil in the margins: "Wonderful!" "Beautiful!" or "Serves him right!"
Lenstchka sang without opening her mouth.

Post coitum: We Balderiovs always excelled in vigor and health.

He drove in a cab, and, as he watched his son walking away, thought: "Perhaps, he belongs to the race of men who will no longer trundle in scurvy cabs, as I do, but will fly through the skies in balloons."

She is so beautiful that it is even frightening; dark eyebrows.

The son says nothing, but the wife feels him to be an enemy; she feels that he has overheard everything. . . .

What a lot of idiots there are among ladies. People get so used to it that they do not notice it.

They often go to the theatre and read serious magazines — and yet are spiteful and immoral.

Nat: "I never have fits of hysterics. I am not a pampered darling." [1]

Nat: (continually to her sisters): "O, how ugly you have grown. O, how old you do look!"

To live one must have something to hang on to. . . . In the provinces only the body works, not the spirit.

You won't become a saint through other people's sins.

Koulyguin: "I am a jolly fellow, I infect every one with my mood."

Koul. Gives lessons at rich houses.

Koul. In Act IV without mustaches.

The wife implores the husband: "Don't get fat."

O if there were a life in which every one grew younger and more beautiful.

---

1 This and the following few passages are from the rough draft of Chekhov's play *Three Sisters*.

Irene: "It is hard to live without a father, without a mother." — "And without a husband." — "Yes, without a husband. Whom could one confide in? To whom could one complain? With whom could one share one's joy? One must love some one strongly."

Koulyguin (to his wife): "I am so happy to be married to you, that I consider it ungentlemanly and improper to speak of or even mention a dowry. Hush, don't say anything. . . ."

The doctor enjoys being at the duel.

It is difficult to live without orderlies. You cannot make the servants answer your bell.

The 2nd, 3rd, and 6th companies left at 4, and we leave at 12 sharp. [1]

In the daytime conversations about the loose manners of the girls in secondary schools, in the evening a lecture on degeneration and the decline of everything, and at night, after all this, one longs to shoot oneself.

In the life of our towns there is no pessimism, no Marxism, and no movements, but there is stagnation, stupidity, mediocrity.

He had a thirst for life, but it seemed to him to mean that he wanted a drink — and he drank wine.

---

1 Here the fragments from the rough draft of *Three Sisters* end.

F. in the town-hall: Sergey Nik. in a plaintive voice: "Gentlemen, where can we get the means? Our town is poor."

To be idle involuntarily means to listen to what is being said, to see what is being done; but he who works and is occupied hears little and sees little.

In the skating rink he raced after L.; he wanted to overtake her and it seemed as if it were life which he wanted to overtake, that life which one cannot bring back or overtake or catch, just as one cannot catch one's shadow.

Only one thought reconciled him to the doctor: just as he had suffered from the doctor's ignorance, so perhaps some one was suffering from his mistakes.

But isn't it strange? In the whole town there is not a single musician, not a single orator, not a prominent man.

Honorable Justice of the Peace, Honorable Member of the Children's Shelter — all honorable.

L. studied and studied — but people who had finished developing could not understand her, nor could the young. *Ut consecutivum.*

He is dark, with little side-whiskers, dressed like a dandy, dark eyes, a warm brunet. He exterminates bugs, talks about earthquakes and China. His fiancée has a dowry of 8,000 roubles; she is very handsome, as her aunt says. He is an agent for a fire-insurance company, etc. "You're awfully pretty, my darling, awfully. And 8,000 into the bargain! You are a beauty; when I looked at you to-day, a shiver ran down my back."

He: Earthquakes are caused by the evaporation of water.

Names: Goose, Pan, Oyster.
"Were I abroad, they would give me a medal for such a surname."

I can't be said to be handsome, but I am rather pretty.

ANTON CHEKHOV'S LETTERS

1882-1904

THE LETTERS

1882 - 1904

To Alex. P. Chekhov
Moscow. April, 1883.

You underscore trifles in your writings, and yet you are
not a subjective writer by nature; it is an acquired trait
in you. To give up this acquired subjectivity is as easy as
to take a drink. One needs only to be more honest, to
throw oneself overboard everywhere, not to obtrude oneself into the hero of one's own novel, to renounce oneself
for at least a half hour. You have a story in which a young
wedded couple kiss all through dinner, grieve without
cause, weep oceans of tears. Not a single sensible word;
nothing but *sentimentality*. And you did not write for
the reader. You wrote because *you* like that sort of chatter. But suppose you were to describe the dinner, how
they ate, what they ate, what the cook was like, how insipid
your hero is, how content with his lazy happiness, how
insipid your heroine is, how funny is her love for this
napkin-bound, sated, overfed goose, — we all like to see
happy, contented people, that is true, — but to describe
them, what *they* said and how many times they kissed is
not enough — you need something else: to free yourself
from the personal expression that a placid honey-happi-
ness produces upon everybody. . . . Subjectivity is a
terrible thing. It is bad in this alone, that it reveals the

author's hands and feet. I'll bet that all priests' daughters
and clerks' wives who read your works are in love with
you, and if you were a German you would get free beer in
all the Bierhalle where the German women serve. If it
were not for this subjectivity you would be the best of
artists. You know how to laugh, sting, and ridicule, you
possess a rounded style, you have experienced much, have
seen so much, — alas! The material is all wasted.

TALENT AND DISCIPLINE

To Alex. P. Chekhov
Moscow.   April 6, 1886.

Respect yourself, for heaven's sake, and don't let your
hand grow slack when your brain grows lazy. Write not
more than two stories a week, and polish them carefully,
so that your work will bear the aspect of work. Do not
invent sufferings that you never experienced, and do not
paint pictures you never saw, for a lie is even more annoying in a story than in a conversation. . . .

I will conclude this sermon by a quotation from a letter
that I recently received from Grigorovich: "Respect your
talent, for it is a rare gift; . . . save your impressions for
careful, thoughtful work, not written at one sitting. . . .
You will at once attract the attention of responsive souls,
and before long of the entire reading public."

Another great authority, Souvorin, writes to me, "When
one writes a great deal, not everything comes out equally
good."

The third great man, our Bilibin, scolds me in his letters
for writing too much. . . .

Leikin is now out of fashion, and I have taken his place in Petrograd. I am now very fashionable here and I should like you to keep up with me.

NATURE AND PSYCHOLOGY

To Alex. P. Chekhov
Babkin. May 10, 1886.

In my opinion a true description of Nature should be very brief and have a character of relevance. Commonplaces such as, "the setting sun bathing in the waves of the darkening sea, poured its purple gold, etc.," — "the swallows flying over the surface of the water twittered merrily," — such commonplaces one ought to abandon. In descriptions of Nature one ought to seize upon the little particulars, grouping them in such a way that, in reading, when you shut your eyes, you get a picture.

For instance, you will get the full effect of a moonlight night if you write that on the mill-dam a little glowing star-point flashed from the neck of a broken bottle, and the round, black shadow of a dog, or a wolf, emerged and ran, etc.* Nature becomes animated if you are not squeamish about employing comparisons of her phenomena with ordinary human activities, etc.

In the sphere of psychology, details are also the thing. God preserve us from commonplaces. Best of all is it to avoid depicting the hero's state of mind; you ought to try

---

* Almost literally a passage later used in the *Sea Gull*.

to make it clear from the hero's actions. It is not necessary to portray many characters. The centre of gravity should be in two persons: him and her. . . .

I write this to you as a reader having a definite taste. Also, in order that you, when writing, may not feel alone. To be alone in work is a hard thing. Better poor criticism than none at all. Is it not so?

ON LITERARY LIFE

To Mme. M. V. Kiselev
Moscow. Sept. 21, 1886.

It is not much fun to be a great writer. To begin with, it's a dreary life. Work from morning till night, and very little to show for it. Money is as scarce as cats' tears. I don't know how it is with Zola and Shchedrin, but in my flat it is cold and smoky. . . .

Nevertheless, authorship has its good points. First, according to the latest reports my book is going well; secondly, in October I shall have money; thirdly, I am beginning little by little to reap laurels: I am pointed out in the refreshment rooms; attentions are shown me, and I am treated to butterbread. Korsh caught sight of me in his theatre, and right off handed me a season ticket. . . . The tailor Bieloüsov bought my book, is reading it aloud at home, and is prophesying a great future for me. My colleagues, the physicians, sigh when they meet me, begin to talk of literature, and assure me that they are tired of medicine, etc.

THE CULTURED MAN

To Nikolai Chekhov
Moscow, 1886.

You often complain that people "don't understand you!" Goethe and Newton did not make this complaint. . . .

I assure you as a brother and as a friend that I understand you and feel for you with all my heart. I know your good qualities as I know my five fingers; I value and deeply respect them. . . .

You have only one fault, and the falseness of your position, and your unhappiness, and your catarrh of the bowels are all due to it. That is, your utter lack of culture. . . . You see, life has its conditions. In order to feel comfortable among educated people, to be at home and happy with them, one must have a certain degree of culture. Talent has brought you into such a circle, you belong to it, but, — you are drawn away from it, and you hover between cultured people and the next-door lodgers.

Cultured people must, in my opinion, fulfill the following conditions:

1. They respect human personality, and for this reason they are always kind, gentle, and ready to give in to others. . . .

2. They have sympathy not alone for beggars and cats. Their heart aches for what the eye does not see.

3. They respect the property of others, and therefore pay their debts.

4. They are sincere, and dread lying as they dread fire. . . . They do not pose; they behave in the streets as they

do at home; they do not show off before their humbler comrades. They are not given to empty babbling, and to forcing their uninvited confidences on other people. Out of respect for others, they more often keep silent than talk.

5. They do not disparage themselves to rouse compassion. They do not play on the strings of other people's hearts so that they may sigh and make much of them. They do not cry "I am misunderstood," or "I have become second-rate," because all this is striving after cheap effect, is low, stale, false. . . .

6. They have no shallow vanity. . . . If they do a pennyworth they do not strut about as though they had done a hundred roubles' worth, and do not brag of having the entry where others are not admitted. . . . The truly talented always keep in obscurity among the crowd, as far as possible from advertisement. . . . Even Kriloff has said that an empty barrel echoes more loudly than a full one.

7. If they have talent they respect it. They sacrifice to it rest, women, wine, vanity. . . . They are proud of their talent. . . . Besides, they are fastidious.

8. They develop the æsthetic feeling in themselves. . . . They seek as far as possible to restrain and ennoble the sexual instinct. . . . What they want in a woman is not a bed-fellow. . . . They want especially, if they are artists, freshness, elegance, humanity, the capacity for motherhood. . . . They do not swill vodka at all hours of the day and night. . . . They drink only when they

are free, on occasion. . . . For they want *mens sana in corpore sano.*

And so on. That is what cultured people are like. In order to be cultured and not to stand below the level of your surroundings it is not enough to have read "The Pickwick Papers," and memorized a monologue from "Faust." . . .

What is needed is constant work, day and night, constant reading, study, will. . . . Every hour is precious for it. . . . Come to us; smash the vodka bottle; lie down and read, — Turgeniev, if you like, whom you have not read.

LITERATURE AND TRUTH

To M. V. Kiselev

January 14, 1887.

Even your praise of "On the Road" has not lessened my anger as an author, and I hasten to avenge myself for what you say about "Mire." Be on your guard, and take firm hold of the back of your chair that you do not faint. Well, here goes.

It is best to meet every critical article with a silent bow, even if it is abusive and unjust — such is the literary etiquette. It is not the correct thing to answer, and all who do so are justly blamed for excessive vanity. But since your criticism is like "an evening conversation on the steps of the Babinko lodge" . . . and as, without touching on the literary aspects of the story, it raises general questions of principle, I shall not be sinning against the etiquette if I allow myself to continue our conversation.

In the first place, I, like you, do not admire literature of the kind we are discussing. As a reader and "a private citizen" I am glad to avoid it, but if you ask my honest and sincere opinion about it, I shall say that it is still an open question whether it has a right to exist, — a question that has as yet not been settled. . . . You and I and the critics of all the world have no such firm certainty as would give us the right to disown this literature. I do not know who is right: Homer, Shakespeare, Lope de Vega, the ancients generally who did not fear to grub in the "dung-hill," but who were more stable in their moral relations than we; or the modern writers, fastidious on paper, but coldly cynical in soul and in their manner of life? I do not know who has bad taste: the Greeks, who were not ashamed to sing such love as really is in beautiful Nature, or the readers of Gaboriau, Marlitt, Per Bobo.* Like the problems of non-resistance to evil, free-will, etc., this question can be settled only in the future. We can only think about it, but to solve it means to go beyond the limits of our competency. Reference to Turgeniev and Tolstoy, who avoided this "dung-hill," does not clear up the question. Their aversion does not prove anything; there were writers before them who not only regarded sordidness as "scoundrelly among scoundrels," but held the same view of descriptions of *muzhiks* and clerks and all beneath the titular rank. And a single period, no matter how brilliant, does not give us the right to draw an inference in favor of this or the other tendency. Nor does reference to the cor-

---

* Boborikin.

rupting influence of a given literary tendency solve the question. Everything in this world is relative and approximate. There are people who will be corrupted even by juvenile literature, who read, with particular pleasure, the piquant passages in the Psalter and the Proverbs of Solomon, while there are those who become the purer the more they know about the evil side of life. Publicists, lawyers, physicians, initiated into all the secret human sins, are not reputed to be immoral; realistic writers are often more moral than archimandrites. And finally, no literature can in its cynicism surpass actual life; a wineglassful will not make drunk the man who has already emptied a whole cask.

2. That the world "swarms with male and female scum" is perfectly true. Human nature is imperfect, and it would, therefore, be strange to find only righteous people on this earth. But to think that the task of literature is to gather the pure grain from the muck heap, is to reject literature itself. Artistic literature is called so just because it depicts life as it really is. Its aim is truth, — unconditional and honest. To narrow down its functions to such a specialty as selecting the "unsullied," is as fatal· to it as to have Levitan paint a tree and to forbid him to include the dirty bark and the yellow leaves. I agree with you that the "cream" is a fine thing, but a litterateur is not a confectioner, not a dealer in cosmetics, not an entertainer; he is a man bound, under compulsion, by the realization of his duty, and by his conscience; having put his hand to the plow he must not plead weakness; and no matter how painful it is to him, he is constrained to overcome his aver-

sion, and soil his imagination with the sordidness of life. He is just like any ordinary reporter. What would you say if a newspaper reporter, because of his fastidiousness or from a wish to give pleasure to his readers, were to describe only honest mayors, high-minded ladies, and virtuous railroad contractors? To a chemist, nothing on earth is unclean. A writer must be as objective as a chemist; he must abandon the subjective line; he must know that dung-heaps play a very respectable part in a landscape, and that evil passions are as inherent in life as good ones.

3. Writers are the children of their age, and therefore, like the rest of the public, ought to surrender to the external conditions of society. Thus, they must be absolutely decent. Only this have we the right to require of the realists. For the rest, you say nothing against the form and execution of "Mire." . . . And so, I take it, I have been decent.

4. I admit that I seldom consult my conscience when I write. This is due to habit and the brief, compressed form of my work. Let us say that when I express this or that opinion about literature, I do not take myself into account.

5. You write: "If I were the editor I would have returned to you this feuilleton for your own good." Why not go further? Why not go for the editors who print such stories? Why not denounce the Administration of the Press for not suppressing immoral newspapers?

The fate of literature would be woeful (both little and great literature) if you left it to the will of individuals. That's the first thing. In the second place, there is no police which we can consider competent in literary matters.

I agree that we must have curbs and whips, for knaves find
their way even into literature, but, think what you will,
you cannot find a better police for literature than criticism
and the author's own conscience. People have been trying
to discover such a police since the creation of the world,
but nothing better has been found. You would wish me
to suffer the loss of one hundred and fifteen roubles and be
censured by the editor. Others, among them your father,
are delighted with the story. Some send letters of reproach
to Souvorin, reviling everything, the newspaper, me, etc.
Who, then, is right? Who is the judge?

6. Further, you write: "Leave such writing to spiritless
and unfortunate scribblers like Okreits,* Pince-nez † or
Aloe." ‡

May Allah pardon me if you wrote those lines sincerely!
To be condescending toward humble people because of
their humbleness does not do honor to the human heart.
In literature, the lower ranks are as necessary as in the
army, — so says the mind, and the heart ought to confirm
this most thoroughly.

STORY PLANS

To A. N. Pleshcheyev
Moscow.   Feb. 9, 1888.

I am in a hurry to start on something short, but I long
for some large work. Oh, if you only knew what a plot for

---

* S. S. Okreits.
† The addressee.
‡ Alexander P. Chekhov.

a novel I have in my mind!   What wonderful women!
What funerals! What marriages! If I had money I would
rush off to the Crimea; I'd sit down under a cypress-tree,
and I'd produce a novel inside of a month or two. I have
already completed three signatures, — can you imagine it!
No, I exaggerate: if I had money to spend freely, then all
the novels would fly to the wind.

When I complete the first part of my novel I shall take
the liberty of sending it to you and not to the *Sieverny
Viestnik,* because my tale is not for the super-censored
magazines.   I am greedy; I like to have crowds in my
works, and that is why my tale is going to be long. And
then the people whom I present are dear and congenial to
me, and I want to be with them longer.

To A. S. Souvorin

Moscow.   1888 (no date).

Ah, what a story I have undertaken! I shall ask you to
read it. The form is literary-feuilletonistic. A respectable
man deprives another respectable man of his wife, and
writes his opinion about it; he lives with her, — his opinion;
he separates from her, — again his opinion.   In the course
of the story I say something about the theatre, about
prejudices, about "dissimilarity of convictions," about
family life and the unfitness of the modern intellectual for
life, about Pechorin, Onegin, and Kazbek.*   It is a fearful
vinaigrette. The wings of my mind are beating, and I
don't know whither to fly.

----

* Pechorin, the hero of Lermontov's A Hero of Our Time; Kasbek, a
mountain in the Caucasus.

THE PRICE OF FAME

To A. S. Souvorin
Moscow.   (No date), 1888.

You say that writers are God's elect. I will not contradict you. Shcheglov calls me the Potemkin of literature, and so it is not for me to speak of the thorny path, of disappointments, and so on. I do not know whether I have ever suffered more than shoemakers, mathematicians, or railway guards do; I do not know who speaks through my lips — God or someone worse. I will allow myself to mention only one little drawback which I have experienced and which you probably know from experience also. It is this. You and I are fond of ordinary people; but other people are fond of us because they think we are not ordinary. Me, for instance, they invite everywhere and regale me with food and drink like a general at a wedding. My sister is indignant that people on all sides invite her simply because she is a writer's sister. Hence it follows that if in the eyes of our friends we should appear to-morrow as ordinary mortals, they will leave off loving us, and will only pity us. And that is unpleasant. It is unpleasant, too, that they like the very things in us which we often dislike and despise in ourselves. It is unpleasant that I was right when I wrote the story, "The First-Class Passenger," in which an engineer and a professor talk about fame.

THE WRITER'S RESPONSIBILITY

To A. S. Souvorin
Sumi. May 30, 1888.

What you say about "Lights" is quite just. You write
that neither the conversation on pessimism, nor the story
of Kisochka helps in the least to solve the problem of
pessimism. It seems to me that the writer of fiction should
not try to solve such questions as those of God, pessimism,
etc. His business is but to describe those who have been
speaking or thinking about God and pessimism, how, and
under what circumstances. The artist should be, not the
judge of his characters and their conversations, but only
an unbiassed witness. I once overheard a desultory conversation about pessimism between two Russians; nothing
was solved, — and my business is to report the conversation exactly as I heard it, and let the jury, — that is, the
readers, estimate its value. My business is merely to be
talented, i.e., to be able to distinguish between important
and unimportant statements, to be able to illuminate the
characters and speak their language. Shcheglov-Leontyev
finds fault with me because I concluded the story with the
phrase: "There's no way of making things out in this
world!" In his opinion an artist-psychologist *must* work
things out, for that is just why he is a psychologist. But
I do not agree with him. The time has come for writers,
especially those who are artists, to admit that in this world
one cannot make anything out, just as Socrates once admitted it, just as Voltaire admitted it. The mob think they

know and understand everything; the more stupid they are, the wider, I think, do they conceive their horizon to be. And if an artist in whom the crowd has faith decides to declare that he understands nothing of what he sees, — this in itself constitutes a considerable clarity in the realm of thought, and a great step forward.

"LITERATURE IS MY MISTRESS . . ."

To A. S. Souvorin
Moscow. September 11, 1888.

. . . You advise me not to hunt after two hares, and not to think of medical work. I do not know why one should not hunt two hares even in the literal sense. . . . I feel more confident and more satisfied with myself when I reflect that I have two professions and not one. Medicine is my lawful wife and literature is my mistress. When I get tired of one I spend the night with the other. Though it's disorderly, it's not so dull, and besides, neither of them loses anything from my infidelity. If I did not have my medical work I doubt if I could have given my leisure and my spare thoughts to literature. There is no discipline in me.

THE GENERAL AND THE PARTICULAR

To A. S. Souvorin
Moscow. Oct. 18, 1888.

If Jesus Christ had been more radical and had said, "Love your enemies as yourself," he would not have said what he wished. Neighbors — it is a general conception, but enemies — a particular matter. The trouble is not that we hate enemies, of whom we have few, but that we do not love sufficiently our neighbors, of whom we have many, many. "Love your enemy as yourself," if you please, Christ would have said had he been a woman. Women like to draw from general conceptions a clear, striking particular. But Christ, standing above enemies, not noticing them, a nature masculine, balanced, and with a wide sweep of thought, gave scarcely any significance to the difference that exists in individuals of the conception "neighbor." You and I are subjective. If we are spoken to, for instance, about animals in general, we at once recall wolves and crocodiles, or nightingales and lovely roebucks; for the zoologist there is no difference between the wolf and the roebuck; for him such difference is too insignificant. You have mastered the understanding of newspaper work to a degree; the particulars that led the public to anger appear to you insignificant. You have acquired for yourself a general understanding, and so you have made a success of newspaper work, but those people who could grasp only particulars have been ruined. . . . In medicine it is exactly the same. He who cannot think medically but judges by particulars, denies medicine; Botkin, Zakharin, Virchow, and Pirogov are, to be sure, undoubtedly clever and gifted people; they believe in medicine as in God, because they grew up in the understanding of "medicine." It is exactly the same in belle-lettres. The expression "tendency" does not have in its essence the meaning of people advancing by particulars.

THE PUSHKIN PRIZE

To A. S. Lazarev-Gruzinsky
Moscow. October 20, 1888.

In my letter I just wished to point out that even great authors may write themselves out, become wearisome; they often commit annoying blunders, and find themselves in a blind alley. I myself am exposed to this danger far more than some others, and you, as a man of sense, will not deny the fact. First of all, I am an unclaimed child of Fate; in literature I am a sort of Potemkin who appeared from the depths of devastation. I am a bourgeois among the nobility, and such people do not last very long; they are like a string that is suddenly drawn taut and snaps. Secondly, the train that keeps going on without a hitch or stop, regardless of weather and the supply of fuel, runs the greatest risk of running off the tracks. . . .

The Pushkin Prize is certainly an important distinction, not for me alone. I am happy that I pointed out to many others the road to the larger magazines, and I rejoice that my gaining the Prize will inspire others with the hope of academic honors and laurels. All that I write will be forgotten in from five to ten years, but the path paved and made easy by me will be forever free and fresh — in this lies my merit.

PROBLEMS AND PURPOSES

To A. S. Souvorin

Moscow.   October 27, 1888.

In conversation with my literary colleagues I always insist that it is not the artist's business to solve problems that require a specialist's knowledge. It is a bad thing if a writer tackles a subject he does not understand. We have specialists for dealing with special questions: it is their business to judge of the commune, of the future, of capitalism, of the evils of drunkenness, of boots, of the diseases of women. An artist must judge only of what he understands, his field is just as limited as that of any other specialist — I repeat this and insist on it always. That in his sphere there are no questions, but only answers, can be maintained only by those who have never written and have had no experience of thinking in images. An artist observes, selects, guesses, combines — and this in itself presupposes a problem: unless he had set himself a problem from the very first there would be nothing to conjecture and nothing to select. To put it briefly, I will end by using the language of psychiatry: if one denies that creative work involves problems and purposes, one must admit that an artist creates without premeditation or intention, in a state of aberration; therefore, if an author boasted to me of having written a novel without a preconceived design, under a sudden inspiration, I should call him mad.

You are right in demanding that an artist should take an intelligent attitude to his work, but you confuse two things: *solving a problem* and *stating a problem correctly*. It is only the second that is obligatory for the artist. In "Anna Karenina" and "Evgeni Onegin" not a single problem is solved, but they satisfy you completely because all the problems in these works are correctly stated. It is the business of the judge to put the right questions, but the answers must be given by the jury according to their own lights.

"THE PARTY"

To A. S. Souvorin
Moscow.   October 27, 1888.

. . . You write that the hero of my "Party" is a character worth developing. Good Lord! I am not a senseless brute, you know; I understand that. I understand that I cut the throats of my characters and spoil them, and that I waste good material. . . . On my conscience, I would gladly have spent six months over the "Party"; I like taking things easy, and see no attraction in publishing in white-hot haste. I would willingly, with pleasure, with feeling, in a leisurely way, describe the *whole* of my hero, describe his state of mind while his wife was in labor, his trial, the unpleasant feeling he has after he is acquitted; I would describe the midwife and the doctors having tea in the middle of the night, I would describe the rain. . . . It would give me nothing but pleasure, because I like to take pains and dawdle. But what am I to do? I begin a story on September 10th with the thought that I must finish it by October 5th at the latest; if I don't I shall fail the editor and be left without money. I let myself go at the beginning and write with an easy mind; but by the time I get to the middle I begin to grow timid and to fear that my story will be too long: I have to remember that the *Sieverny Viestnik* has not much money, and that I am one of their expensive contributors. This is why the beginning of my stories is always very promising and looks as though I were starting on a novel, the middle is huddled and timid, and the end is, as in a short sketch, like fireworks. And so in planning a story one is bound to think first about its framework: from a crowd of leading or subordinate characters one selects one person only — wife or husband; one puts him on the canvas and paints him alone, making him prominent, while the others one scatters over the canvas like small coin, and the result is something like the vault of heaven: one big moon and a number of very small stars around it. But the moon is not a success, because it can only be understood if the stars too are intelligible, and the stars are not worked out. And so what I produce is not literature, but something like the patching of Trishka's coat.* What am I to do? I don't know, I don't know. I must trust to time which heals all things.

Speaking on my conscience again, I have not yet begun my literary work, though I have received a literary prize. Subjects for five stories and two novels are languishing in my head. One of the novels was thought of long ago, and some of the characters have grown old without manag-

---
* The reference is to Kriloff's fable *Trishka's Coat*.

ing to get themselves written. In my head there is a whole army of people asking to be let out and waiting for the word of command. All that I have written so far is rubbish in comparison with what I should like to write and should write with rapture. It is all the same to me whether I write "The Party" or "Lights," or a vaudeville or a letter to a friend — it is all dull, spiritless, mechanical, and I get annoyed with critics who attach any importance to "Lights," for instance. I fancy that I deceive them with my work just as I deceive many people with my face, which looks serious or overcheerful. I don't like being successful; the subjects which sit in my head are annoyed, jealous of what has already been written. I am vexed that the rubbish has been done and the good things lie about in the lumber-room like old books. Of course, in thus lamenting I rather exaggerate, and much of what I say is only my fancy, but there is something of the truth in it, a good big part of it. What do I call good? The images which seem best to me, which I love and jealously guard lest I spend and spoil them for the sake of some "Party" written against time. . . . If my love is mistaken, I am wrong, but then it may not be mistaken! I am either a fool and a conceited fellow or I really am an organism capable of being a good writer. All that I now write displeases and bores me, but what sits in my head interests, excites, and moves me — from which I conclude that everybody does the wrong thing and I alone know the secret of doing the right one. Most likely all writers think that. But the devil himself would break his neck at these problems.

Money will not help me to decide what I am to do and how I am to act. An extra thousand roubles will not settle matters, and a hundred thousand is a castle in the air. Besides, when I have money — it may be because I am not accustomed to it, I don't know — I become extremely careless and idle; the sea seems only knee-deep to me then. . . . I need time and solitude.

ON THEATRE

To A. S. Souvorin
Moscow. Nov. 7, 1888.

. . . It is not the public that is to blame for our theatres being so wretched. The public is always and everywhere the same: intelligent and stupid, sympathetic and pitiless, according to mood. It has always been a flock which needs good shepherds and dogs, and it has always gone in the direction in which the shepherds and the dogs drove it. You are indignant that it laughs at flat witticisms and applauds sounding phrases; but then the very same stupid public fills the house to hear "Othello," and, listening to the opera "Evgeni Onegin," weeps when Tatyana writes her letter. . . . The public, however stupid, is generally more clever, more sincere and sympathetic than K—— and the actors, — and these latter think they are the brighter: reciprocal misunderstandings.

THE SCIENTIFIC METHOD

To A. S. Souvorin
Moscow. November, 1888. ·
In the November number of the *Sieverny Viestnik* there

is an article by the poet Merezhkovsky about your humble
servant. It is a long article. I commend to your attention
the end of it; it is characteristic. Merezhkovsky is still
very young, a student — of science I believe. Those who
have assimilated the wisdom of the scientific method and
learned to think scientifically experience many alluring
temptations. Archimedes wanted to turn the earth round,
and the presentday hot-heads want by science to conceive
the inconceivable, to discover the physical laws of creative
art, to detect the laws and the formulæ which are instinctively felt by the artist and are followed by him in creating
music, novels, pictures, etc. Such formulæ probably exist
in nature. We know that A, B, C, do, re, mi, fa, sol, are
found in nature, and so are curves, straight lines, circles,
squares, green, blue, and red. . . . We know that in certain combinations all this produces a melody, or a poem, or
a picture, just as simple chemical substances in certain combinations produce a tree, or a stone, or the sea; but all we
know is that the combination exists, while the law of it is
hidden from us. Those who are masters of the scientific
method feel in their souls that a piece of music and a tree
have something in common, that both are built up in ac-
cordance with equally uniform and simple laws. Hence the
question: What are these laws? And hence the temptation
to work out a physiology of creative art (like Boborikin),
or in the case of younger and more diffident writers, to
base their arguments on nature and on the laws of nature
(Merezhkovsky). There probably is such a thing as the
physiology of creative art, but we must nip in the bud our
dreams of discovering it. If the critics take up a scientific

attitude no good will come of it: they will waste a dozen years, write a lot of rubbish, make the subject more obscure than ever — and nothing more. It is always a good thing to think scientifically, but the trouble is that scientific thinking about creative art will be bound to degenerate in the end into searching for the "cells" or the "centers" which control the creative faculty.   Some stolid German will discover these cells somewhere in the occipital lobes, another German will agree with him, a third will disagree, and a Russian will glance through the article about the cells and reel off an essay about it in the *Sieverny Viestnik*.   The *Viestnik Evropi* will criticize the essay, and for three years there will be in Russia an epidemic of nonsense which will give money and popularity to blockheads and do nothing but irritate intelligent people.

For those who are obsessed with the scientific method and to whom God has given the rare talent of thinking scientifically, there is to my mind only one way out — the philosophy of creative art. One might collect together all the best works of art that have been produced throughout the ages and, with the help of the scientific method, discover the *common* element in them which makes them like one another and conditions their value.   That *common* element will be the law. There is a great deal that works which are called immortal have in common; if this common element were excluded from each of them, a work would lose its charm and its value.   So that this universal something is necessary, and is the *Conditio sine qua non* of every work that claims to be immortal.   It is of more use to young people to write critical articles than poetry.

Merezhkovsky writes smoothly and youthfully, but at
every page he loses heart, makes reservations and conces-
sions, and this means that he is not clear upon the subject. He calls me a poet, he styles my stories "novelli"
and my heroes "failures" — that is, he follows the beaten
track. It is time to give up these "failures," superfluous
people, etc., and to think of something original. Merezhkovsky calls my monk who composes the songs of praise a
failure. But how is he a failure? God grant us all a life
like his: he believed in God, and he had enough to eat
and he had the gift of composing poetry. . . . To divide men into the successful and the unsuccessful is to
look at human nature from a narrow, preconceived point
of view. Are you a success or not? Am I? Was Napoleon? Is your servant, Vassily? What is the criterion?
One must be a god to be able to tell successes from failures
without making a mistake.

CRITICS AND CRITICISM

To A. S. Souvorin
Moscow. Dec. 23, 1888.
I read your play again.* There is much that is good
and original in it, that dramatic literature has not had
before, but there are also things that are not so good, i.e.,
in the language. Its merits and faults make up wealth that
one could dwell upon, if we had critics. But this wealth
will lie idle and unproductive until it goes out of date. . . .
There are no critics. There are spouters like the trite

* *Tatyana Repina.*

Tatishchev, the donkey Mikhnevich, and the unconcerned Burenin, — here you have the whole of the Russian critical force. And to write for this force is a thankless job, just as it is to send flowers to one who has a cold in the head.

There are moments when I completely lose heart. For whom and for what do I write? For the public? But I don't see it, and believe in it less than I do in spooks; it is uneducated, badly brought up, and its best elements are unfair and insincere to us. I cannot make out whether this public wants me or not. Burenin says that it does not, and that I waste my time on trifles; the Academy has given me a prize. The devil himself could not make head or tail of it. Write for the sake of money? But I never have any money, and not being used to having it I am almost indifferent to it. For the sake of money I work apathetically. Write for the sake of praise? But praise merely irritates me. Literary society, students, Pleshcheyev, young ladies, etc., were enthusiastic in their praise of my "Nervous Breakdown," but Grigorovich is the only one who has noticed the description of the first snow. And so on, and so on. If we had critics I should know that I provide material, whether good or bad does not matter — that to men who devote themselves to the study of life I am as necessary as a star is to an astronomer. And then I would take trouble over my work and should know what I was working for. But as it is you, I, Muravlin, and the rest are like lunatics who write books and plays to please themselves. To please oneself is, of course, an excellent thing; one feels the pleasure while one is writing, but afterwards? In short, I am sorry for Tatyana Repina, not because she

poisoned herself, but because she lived for life, died in
agony, and was described absolutely to no purpose, without any good to anyone. A number of tribes, religions, lan-
guages, civilizations, have vanished without a trace, vanished because there were no historians or biologists.   In
the same way a number of lives and works of art disappear
before our very eyes owing to the complete absence of
criticism. It may be objected that critics would have nothing to do because all modern works are poor and insignificant. But this is a narrow way of looking at things.   Life
must be studied not from the pluses alone, but from the
minuses too. The conviction that the "eighties" have not
produced a single writer may in itself provide material for
five volumes. . . . I settled down last night to write a
tale for the *Novoe Vremya*, but a woman appeared and
dragged me to see the poet Palmin who, when he was
drunk, had fallen and cut his forehead to the bone.   I was
busy over the drunken fellow for nearly two hours, was
tired out, began to smell of iodoform all over, felt cross,
and came home exhausted. . . . Altogether my life is a
dreary one, and I begin to get fits of hating people, which
used never to happen to me before. Long, stupid conversations, visitors, people asking for help, and helping them
to the extent of one or two or three roubles, spending
money on cabs for the sake of patients who do not pay me
a penny — altogether it is such a hodge-podge that I feel
like running away from home. People borrow money from
me and don't pay it back, they take my books, they waste
my time. . . . Blighted love is the one thing that is
missing.

HAZARDS OF THE STAGE

To A. S. Souvorin
Moscow. Jan. 4, 1889.

You write that the stage lures you because it resembles life. . . . Is this so? But I think that the theatre lures you and me and shrivels Shcheglov up, because it is a form of sport. Where there is success or failure there is sport and hazard.

I should like to have my play staged. What author would not wish that? The main thing, of course, is the money, but the details, too, are interesting. I, for example, can feel very gay at the thought that Anna Ivanovna will be ironical over my success or failure and my inability to greet people; that during the first performance Shcheglov and other friends of mine will seem to me mysterious physiognomies; that all the brunettes sitting in the loges will appear to me to be in a hostile mood; that the Mikhneviches will pass like shades with cheeks red from suffocation and inner tension; that Grigorovich, after the first act, will shout, "Author! Author!" while the author, after the second act, will already feel a weariness in his shoulders, a dryness in the throat, and a desire to go home; I am gay at the thought that, returning from the theatre, I shall hear of a mass of insertions and corrections that I should have made, will hear that Varlamov was good, Davidov dry, Savina dear, (but angry with Dalmatov, who this time stepped on the little finger of her left hand). Gay, because Anna Ivanovna * will finally turn to me, speaking least of all of the play, and will say, "How you have tried me with your play! The whole day the same thing, the same thing. . . . There are no people so dreary as you writers!"

And I will wish her good-night, will go home, drink some wine, and go to bed.

To A. N. Pleshcheyev
Moscow. Jan. 15, 1889.

To write a good play for the theatre one must have special talent; you can be an excellent belletrist and at the same time write patch-work plays; to write a poor play and then change it into a good one, — to take a new focus, cross out, add, insert monologues, revive the dead, and bury the living, — for this is required much greater talent. It is just as hard as it is to buy an old pair of soldier's trousers and try, at all costs, to make a frock-coat of them.

"A DREARY STORY"

To A. S. Souvorin
Moscow. March 11, 1889.

I am writing a novel! I keep writing and writing and I don't see the end of it all. I started at the beginning once more, carefully correcting and abridging everything that had already been written. I have already sketched nine figures, clearly and amply. What a plot! I call the

---

* Madame Souvorin.

novel simply, "Stories from the Life of My Friends." I am writing it in the form of separate, complete stories, closely connected by the common plot, idea, and characters. Each separate story has its own title. Do not imagine that the novel will consist of independent pieces. No, — it is a regular novel, an entity, in which each figure is organically necessary. Grigorovich, to whom you handed the first chapter, expressed doubts about the fact that in it there is a student who is doomed to die, and therefore will not last through the entire novel, i.e., he is superfluous. But this student is just one nail driven into the heel of a large boot. He is a detail, incidental. It will not be easy to master the technique. The work is still weak in this respect, and I fear that there are many mistakes. It will be long-winded, I fear, and will contain foolish things. But I try to avoid dealing with unfaithful wives, suicides, fights, virtuous peasants, devoted servants, clever old women, provincial wits, red-nosed captains, and "new" people, though in some places I fall foul of this last species.

To A. N. Pleshcheyev
Moscow. April 9, 1889.

The novel, after making remarkable progress, is now stranded, waiting for the tide. . . . In the structure of the novel I weave in the life of good people, their fate, deeds, words, ideas, and hopes. My goal is to kill two birds with one stone: to paint life in its true aspects, and to show how far this life falls short of the ideal life. I don't know what this ideal life is, just as it is unknown to all of us. We all know what a dishonest deed is, but

who has looked upon the face of honor?   I shall keep to
the truth that is nearest my heart and which has been
tested by men stronger and wiser than I am.   This truth
is the absolute freedom of man, freedom from oppression,
from prejudices, ignorance, passions, etc.

STAGNATION

To A. S. Souvorin
Moscow.   May 4, 1889.

Nature reconciles man, that is, makes him indifferent.
And in this world one must be indifferent. Only those who
are unconcerned are able to see things clearly, to be just,
and to work. Of course, this includes only thoughtful and
noble people; egoists and empty folk are indifferent enough
as it is.

You say I have grown lazy. That does not mean that
I am now lazier than I used to be.   I work nowadays as
much as I did three or five years ago.   To work, and to
look as though I were working constantly from nine in the
morning till dinner, and after the evening meal until bed-
time, has become a habit with me, and in that respect I
am exactly like a government clerk.   And if my work does
not result in two novels a month or in an income of ten
thousand roubles, it is not my laziness that is to blame,
but my inborn psychological peculiarities.   I do not care
enough for money to make a success of medicine, and for
literature I have not enough passion, and therefore not
enough talent.   The fire burns in me slowly and evenly,

without sudden spluttering and flaring up. And this is why I cannot cover reams of paper each night, or be so carried away by my work that it keeps me from bed when I am sleepy; this is why I commit no particular follies, or accomplish anything very wise.

I am afraid that in this respect I resemble Goncharov, whom I don't like, who is ten heads taller than I am in talent. I have not enough passion; add to that this sort of lunacy: for the last two years I have for no reason at all ceased to care about seeing my work in print, have become indifferent to reviews, to literary conversations, to gossip, to success and failure, to good pay — in short, I have gone downright silly. There is a sort of stagnation in my soul. I explain it by the stagnation in my personal life. I am not disappointed, I am not tired, I am not depressed, but simply, everything has suddenly become less interesting. I must do something to rouse myself.

"A DREARY STORY"

To A. N. Pleshcheyev
Moscow. Sept. 24, 1889.

The name of my tale is "A Dreary Story" (From the Diary of an Old Man). The dullest thing in it, as you see, is the long discussions, which unfortunately, I cannot omit because my hero who writes the notes cannot be without them. These discussions are fated, and as necessary as a heavy gun-carriage to a cannon. They characterize the hero and his temperament, and his constant evasions, even to himself.

To A. N. Pleshcheyev
Moscow. Sept. 30, 1889.

. . . I do not think I ought to change the title of the story. The wags who will, as you foretell, make jokes about "A Dreary Story," are so dull that one need not fear them; and if someone makes a good joke I shall be glad to have given him the occasion for it. The professor could not write about Katya's husband because he did not know him, and Katya does not say anything about him; besides, one of my hero's chief characteristics is that he cares far too little about the inner life of those who surround him, and while people around him are weeping, making mistakes, telling lies, he calmly talks about the theatre or literature. Were he a different sort of man, Liza and Katya might not have come to grief. Yes, the story of Katya's past appears long and dull. But one could not help it. Had I tried to make this section more interesting, then, you will see, my story would have been twice as long. . . .

The short story, like the stage, has its conventions. My instinct tells me that at the end of a novel or a story I must artfully concentrate for the reader an impression of the entire work, and therefore must casually mention something about those whom I have already presented. Perhaps I am in error.

POLITICAL TENDENCIES

To A. N. Pleshcheyev
Moscow. Oct., 1889.

I am afraid of those who look for a tendency between
the lines, and who are determined to regard me either as
a liberal or as a conservative. I am not a liberal, not a
conservative, not a believer in gradual progress, not a
monk, not an indifferentist. I should like to be a free
artist and nothing more, and I regret that God has not
given me the power to be one. I hate lying and violence
in all their forms, and am equally repelled by the secretaries
of consistories and by Notovich and Gradovsky. Pharisaism, stupidity, and despotism reign not in merchants'
houses and prisons alone. I see them in science, in literature, in the younger generation. . . . That is why I have
no preference either for gendarmes, or for butchers, or for
scientists, or for writers, or for the younger generation. I
regard trade-marks and labels as a superstition. My holy
of holies is the human body, health, intelligence, talent,
inspiration, love, and the most absolute freedom — freedom from violence and lying, whatever forms they may
take. This is the program I would follow if I were a great
artist.

ECONOMIC PRESSURE

To A. S. Souvorin
Moscow. December, 1889.

When, the other day, I read "A Family Tragedy" by

Byezhetsky, the story aroused in me something like a feeling of fellow-suffering with the author. Just such a feeling I experience when I see my own books. The justice
in this emotion is about the size of a fly, but my sensitive-
ness and my dependence on the work of others, swell it out
to the proportions of an elephant. I want awfully to hide
myself somewhere for about five years, and occupy myself
with minute, serious work. I must study, study everything
from the beginning, for I, as a litterateur, am a mass of
ignorance. I must write conscientiously, with feeling,
with meaning, write not five sheets of print a month, but
one sheet in five months. I must leave this house, begin
to live at the rate of 700-900 roubles a year instead of
3-4 thousand a year, as now, and I must renounce much
— but in me there is more of Little Russian laziness than
of daring.

T O L S T O Y

To A. N. Pleshcheyev
Moscow. Feb. 15, 1890.

So you really do not like "The Kreutzer Sonata"? I do
not go so far as to say that it is an immortal work of genius,
— I am no judge of that; but, in my opinion, in the whole
mass of that which is now being written, here and abroad,
it is difficult to find its equal both for the importance of
the idea and the beauty of expression. Not to speak of the
artistic merits, which are at times astonishing, the novel
deserves high praise if only for being so stimulating to
thought. On reading it one can hardly refrain from ex-

claiming: "This is true!" or "This is preposterous!" True, it has some very annoying defects. Besides those you mention there is another thing for which one does not feel like forgiving the author, namely, the boldness with which Tolstoy treats that which he does not know and which he refuses to understand, out of sheer stubbornness. Thus, his statements about syphilis, about asylums for children, about women's aversion to copulation, etc., are not only open to dispute, but they actually betray an ignorant man who, in the course of his long life, has not taken the trouble to read two or three pamphlets written by specialists. And yet all these defects scatter like feathers before the wind; one simply does not take account of them in view of the merits of the novel, and if one does notice them it is only with regret that the novel did not escape the lot of all human enterprises, none of which is perfect or free from blemish.

To A. S. Souvorin
Moscow.   March 22, 1890.

. . . Yesterday a young lady told me that Professor Storozhenko had related to her the following anecdote. The Sovereign liked "The Kreutzer Sonata." Pobyedonostsev, Lubimov, and the other cherubim and seraphim, hastened to justify their attitude to Tolstoy by showing his Majesty "Nikolay Palkin." After reading it, his Majesty was so furious that he ordered measures to be taken. Prince Dolgorukov was informed. And so one fine day an adjutant from Dolgorukov comes to Tolstoy and invites him to go at once to the prince. The latter replies: "Tell the

prince that I only visit the houses of my acquaintances."
The adjutant, overcome with confusion, rides away, and
next day brings Tolstoy the official notice demanding from
him an explanation in regard to his "Nikolay Palkin."
Tolstoy reads the document and says:

"Tell his excellency that I have not for a long time past
written anything for publication; I write only for my
friends, and if my friends spread my writings abroad,
they are responsible and not I. Tell him that!"

"But I can't tell him that," cried the adjutant in horror,
"the prince will not believe me!"

"The prince will not believe his subordinates? That's
bad."

Two days later the adjutant comes again with a fresh
document, and learns that Tolstoy has gone away to
Yasnaya Polyana. That is the end of the anecdote.

MORALITY AND ART

To L. Shcheglov
Moscow.   March 22, 1890.

Greetings, dear Jean! Thanks for your long letter and
for the good will that fills it from beginning to end. I shall
be delighted to read your military story. Will it come
out in the Easter number? You write that you feel like
quarreling with me bitterly, "especially on the questions of
morality and art." You speak vaguely of some crimes that
I have committed and that deserve friendly reproaches, and
you even threaten me with "influential newspaper criticism." If we cross out the word "art," the whole sentence

in quotation-marks becomes clearer, but it acquires a meaning that, to speak frankly, puzzles me not a little.   Jean
what is it? How shall I understand it? Is it possible that
I differ in my conception of morality from such people as
you, and even so widely that I deserve reproach and the
special attention of a weighty critique? I cannot think that
you have in mind some unusual, higher morality, because
there are no higher or lower or medium moralities, but
there is only one, namely, that which Jesus Christ gave us
in olden times, and which now prevents me, you, and
Barantsevich from stealing, lying, insulting, etc.   And I,
throughout my whole life, if I am to trust the tranquillity
of my conscience, either by word, or deed, or thought, or
in stories or in playlets, coveted not my neighbor's wife,
or his slave, or his ox, or any of his cattle; I did not steal,
or bear false witness, or flatter the strong and seek favors
of them, nor did I swindle or live as a *souteneur*.   It is
true, in laziness have I spent my days, laughed thought-
lessly, overate, overdrank, lived wantonly, but all this is
personal and does not deprive me of the right to think that
as far as morality is concerned I do not differ from ordinary people either in pluses or in minuses.   No vile deeds
and no glorious exploits — I am just like the majority.
Many sins there are, but with morality I am quits, for I
pay with interest for my sins by those inconveniences which
they bring in their train.   But if you want to quarrel with
me bitterly because I am not a hero, then throw your bit-
terness out of the window and change your scolding into
your dear, tragic laughter, — that is much better.

And as regards the word "art," I fear it as merchants'

wives fear a Sodom rain of brimstone. When people talk to me of the artistic and the anti-artistic, of that which is theatric and non-theatric, of tendency, realism, etc., I become confused, consent irresolutely, and answer with platitudinous half-truths that are not worth a penny. I divide all literary works into two classes: those that I like and those that I do not like. I have no other criterion, and if you were to ask me why I like Shakespeare and dislike Zlatovratsky, I should be unable to answer. Perhaps in time, when I become wiser, I shall acquire a criterion, but meanwhile, all this talk about "artistry" only tires me and seems to me only the continuation of the same scholastic discourses with which people wearied themselves in the Middle Ages.

If the critique, to whose authority you refer, knows that which you and I do not know, why then has it kept silent all this time, why does it not unveil for us the truths and immutable laws? If it knew, believe me, it would have shown us the way long ago, and we would know what to do, and Fofanov would not be in the insane asylum, Garshin would be among the living, Barantsevich would not have the spleen, and we would not be so bored and blue, and you would not yearn for the theatre and I for Sakhalin. But the critique preserves its grave silence, or evades the big things with idle, contemptible chatter. If it seems to you influential, it is only because it is stupid, immodest, insolent, and noisy, because it is an empty barrel to which one listens when one cannot stop its rolling.

Well, let's drop all this and let's sing a different tune. Please do not attach any literary hopes to my trip to Sakhalin. I am going there not for the sake of observations or impressions, but simply in order to live for half a year among new things and in a different way. Place no hopes in me, old man. If I have time enough and prove able to do something, — thank God; if not, — do not blame me.

. . .

THE TECHNIQUE OF OBJECTIVITY

To A. S. Souvorin
Moscow.   April 1, 1890.

You abuse me for objectivity, calling it indifference to good and evil, lack of ideals and ideas, and so on. You would have me, when I describe horse-thieves, say: "Stealing horses is an evil." But that has been known for ages without my saying so. Let the jury judge them; it's my job simply to show what sort of people they are. I write: you are dealing with horse-thieves, so let me tell you that they are not beggars but well-fed people, that they are people of a special cult, and that horse-stealing is not simply theft but a passion. Of course it would be pleasant to combine art with a sermon, but for me personally it is extremely difficult and almost impossible, owing to the conditions of technique. You see, to depict horse-thieves in seven hundred lines I must all the time speak and think in their tone and feel in their spirit, otherwise, if I introduce subjectivity, the image becomes blurred and the story will not be as compact as all short stories ought to be. When I write, I reckon entirely upon the reader to add for himself the subjective elements that are lacking in the story.

TOLSTOY

To A. S. Souvorin

Moscow.   Sept. 8, 1891.

Tolstoy calls our having money and eating meat lying —
that's too much. . . .

Tolstoy denies mankind immortality, but my God! how
much that is personal there is in it! The day before yesterday I read his "Afterword." Strike me dead! but it
is stupider and stuffier than "Letters to a Governor's
Wife," which I despise. The devil takes the philosophy of
the great ones of this world! All the great sages are as
despotic as generals, and as ignorant and as indelicate as
generals, because they feel secure. Diogenes spat in people's faces, knowing that he would not suffer for it. Tolstoy
abuses doctors as scoundrels, and displays his ignorance
in great questions because he's just such a Diogenes who
won't be locked up or abused in the newspapers. And so
to the devil with the philosophy of all the great ones of
this world! The whole of it with its fanatical "After-
words" and "Letters to a Governor's Wife" is not worth
one little mare in his "Story of a Horse." . . .

To A. S. Souvorin

Moscow.   Oct. 25, 1891.

Every night I stay awake and read "War and Peace."
One reads with as much curiosity and naïve wonder as
though one were reading the book for the first time. Re-
markably good. Only, I don't like those parts where

Napoleon appears. As soon as Napoleon is taken up, we get a forcing of effect and a distortion to show that he was more stupid than he actually was. All that Pierre, Prince Andrei, or the altogether worthless Nikolai Rostov say and do — all that is good, clever, substantial and stirring; all, on the other hand, that Napoleon thinks and says is not substantial or clever; it is turgid, and bears no relation to the meaning of the tale.

.   .   .   .

If I had been with Prince Andrei I would have cured him. It is strange to read that the wound of the prince, a rich man who was treated day and night by a physician, and who had the benefit of the nursing of Natasha and Sonya, should have given forth a putrid odor. In what a wretched state was the science of medicine in those days! Tolstoy, in writing this bulky novel, could not help maintaining to the end his abhorrence of medicine.

To A. S. Souvorin
Moscow. Dec. 11, 1891.

Oh, that Tolstoy, that Tolstoy! He, at the present time, is not a human being, but a superman, a Jupiter. In the *Shornik* he offers an article on diet, and the whole article consists of advice and practical suggestions to such a degree intelligent, simple, and reasonable, that, in the words of the editor of the *Russkiya Viedomosti*, Sobolevsky, the article should have appeared not in the *Shornik*, but in the *Government Gazette*.

"WARD NO. 6"

To. A. S. Souvorin
Station Lopasnya.   March 31, 1892.

I am leading the life of a privileged vegetable which is constantly poisoned by the thought that it must write, eternally write. I am writing a story. Before publishing it, I should like to send it to you for correction — for your opinion is golden to me — but it is necessary to hurry, as there is no money. In the story there is much reasoning, and a complete absence of a love-element. There is a fable, a plot, and a dénouement. The tendency is liberal. Two full signatures of print. But it would have been well to talk it over with you; I am afraid that I deal with nonsense and tiresome things. You have a surpassing taste, and I believe in your first impression as surely as I do that there is a sun in the heavens. If they do not hurry the printing of my story, and give me a month or two for revisions, then permit me to send you the proofs. Nowadays this precaution is necessary. If Jean Shcheglov would have sent his wild, fantastic novel, "Near the Truth," to you or me for revision before turning it over to the printer, it would, probably, not have aroused so much adverse criticism. Living isolated in a selfish shell, and taking part only indirectly in the intellectual life of the day, one is likely to write all sorts of nonsense, without realizing it.

ROUBLES AND KOPECKS

To A. S. Souvorin
Station Lopasnya.   June 16, 1892.

. . . You want me to write you my impressions. My soul longs for breadth and altitude, but I am forced to lead a narrow life spent over trashy roubles and kopecks. There is nothing more vulgar than a petty bourgeois life with its halfpence, its victuals, its futile talk, and its useless conventional virtue; my heart aches from the consciousness that I am working for money, and money is the center of all I do. This aching feeling, together with a sense of justice, makes my writing a contemptible pursuit in my eyes: I don't respect what I write, I am apathetic and bored with myself, and glad that I have medicine which, anyway, I practise not for the sake of money. I ought to have a bath in sulphuric acid and flay off my skin, and then grow a new hide. . . .

"LIFE FOR LIFE'S SAKE"

To A. S. Souvorin
Melikhovo.   Dec. 3, 1892.

That the modern generation of writers and artists has no aim in its creation, is an altogether legitimate thing, consequent and interesting, and if S. was not frightened by the fact and its consequences, by sulphur and brimstone, it does not mean that I was sly in my letter, and hid my soul. You yourself showed a certain insincerity even after she wrote to you, otherwise you would not have sent her my letter. In my letters to you I am often naïve and not always in the right, but I never write what is not in my heart.

If you want insincerity, there are a million *poods* of it in S.'s letter. "The greatest wonder is man himself, and we shall never tire of studying him . . .", or, "The aim of life . . . is life itself . . .", or, "I believe in life, in its bright moments, for which we not only can, but must live; I believe in man, in the good part of his soul," etc. Is all this really sincere, and does it mean anything? It is not an opinion, but mere gabble. She underscores "can" and "must," because she is afraid to talk of that which is, and of which one must take account. Let her in the beginning say what there is, and then I will listen to what can and must be. She believes in "life," and that means that she believes in nothing if she is clever, — or that she believes in the God of the *muzhiks*, and crosses herself in the dark, if she is a grandma.

Under the influence of her letter you write me about "life for life's sake." I sincerely thank you. But her letter with its joy of life is a thousand times more nearly like a grave than mine. I write that there are no aims, and you understand that I consider these aims necessary, and would gladly go out to seek them, — and S. writes that it is not right to fool people with talk about all kinds of blessings that they will never get, . . . "that which is, is valuable," and in her opinion our whole misfortune lies in our always looking for some higher, transcendental aims. If that is not woman's logic it certainly is a hopeless philosophy. He who sincerely thinks that higher, transcendental aims are as little necessary to man as to a cow, that in these aims lies our whole misfortune, — for him there is left only to eat, drink, sleep, or, when he grows sick of all that, to go and smash his head on the edge of his trunk.

I do not reproach S., but only want to say that she is not, by far, a person aware of the joy of living. Evidently, she is a good lady; nevertheless, you showed her my letter in vain. She is a stranger to me, and now I find myself in an awkward situation.

ON TALENT

To I. I. Ostrovsky
Station Lopasnya. Feb. 11, 1893.

The older I become, the less and the more lazily I work. I already feel old age. My health is not what it might be. As regards pantheism, about which you wrote me several nice words, I will say this: eyes do not grow above the forehead; every one writes as he can. I would gladly soar up to Heaven, but I have not the strength. If the nature of literary work depended only upon the good will of the author, then, you may believe it, we would count good writers by the tens and hundreds. It is not a matter of pantheism, but of the degree of talent.

"THE BLACK MONK"

To A. S. Souvorin
Melikhovo. January 25, 1894.

I believe I am mentally sound. It is true I have no

special desire to live, but that is not, so far, disease, but something probably passing and natural. It does not follow every time that an author describes someone mentally deranged, that he is himself deranged. I wrote "The Black Monk" without any melancholy ideas, through cool reflection. I simply had a desire to describe megalomania. The monk floating across the country was a dream, and when I woke I told Misha * about it. So you can tell Anna Ivanovna† that poor Anton Pavlovich, thank God! has not gone out of his mind yet, but that he eats a great deal at supper, and so he dreams of monks.

"INEXORABLE, IMPLACABLE WORK . . ."

To Mme. L. S. Mizinov
Yalta. March 27, 1894.

Not for one moment does the thought leave me that I must, that I am obliged to write. To write, and write, and write. I am of the opinion that inner happiness is impossible without idleness. My ideal: to be idle and love a fat girl. For me the greatest delight is to walk, or to sit and do nothing; my favorite occupation, — to collect what is not needed (papers, bits of straw, etc.), and to do useless things. Meanwhile I am a litterateur, and must write, even here in Yalta. Dear Lika, when you become a big girl, and are given a huge allowance, then be so good as to marry me and feed me at your cost, so that I may do nothing. And if you are really going to die, then let

---

* His brother Mikhail.
† The addressee's wife.

Varya Eberlai do this for me; I like her, as you know.
I am so shattered by the constant thought of inexorable,
implacable work, that it is already a week since I have
been tortured by ceaseless palpitations of the heart.   A
horrible sensation.

TOLSTOY'S MORALITY

To A. S. Souvorin
Yalta.   March 27, 1894.

Since I have quite given up smoking I have been free
from gloomy and anxious moods.   Perhaps because I am
not smoking, Tolstoy's morality has ceased to touch me;
at the bottom of my heart I take up a hostile attitude
towards it, and that of course is not just.   I have peasant
blood in my veins, and you won't astonish me with peasant
virtues.   From my childhood I have believed in progress,
and I could not help believing in it since the difference between the time when I used to be thrashed and when they
gave up thrashing me was tremendous. . . . But Tolstoy's
philosophy touched me profoundly and took possession of
me for six or seven years, and what affected me was not
its general propositions, with which I was familiar before
hand, but Tolstoy's manner of expressing it, his reasonable-
ness, and probably a sort of hypnotism.   Now something
in me protests, reason and justice tell me that in the electricity and heat of love for man there is something greater
than chastity and abstinence from meat.   War is an evil
and legal justice is an evil; but it does not follow from that
that I ought to wear bark shoes and sleep on the stove

with the laborer, and so on, and so on. But that is not the point; it is not a matter of *pro and con;* the thing is that one way or another Tolstoy has passed for me; he is not in my soul, and he has departed from me, saying: "I leave this your house empty." I am untenanted. I am sick of theorizing of all sorts, and such bounders as Max Nordau I read with positive disgust. Patients in a fever do not want food, but they do want something, and that vague craving they express as "longing for something sour." I, too, want something sour, and that's not a mere chance feeling, for I notice the same mood in others around me. It is just as if they had all been in love, had fallen out of love, and now were looking for some new distraction. It is very possible and very likely that the Russians will pass through another period of enthusiasm for the natural sciences, and that the materialistic movement will be fashionable. Natural science is performing miracles now. And it may act upon people like Mamay,* and dominate them by its mass and grandeur. All that is in the hands of God, however. And theorizing about it makes one's head go round.

ON VERSE

To A. V. Zhirkevich
Station Lopasnya. March, 1895.

Verse is not in my line. I have never written poetry; my mind refuses to memorize poetry, and I can only take hold of it like a *muzhik,* but I cannot state definitely why

------

* The Tatar chieftain, who conquered Russia.

it pleases me or wearies me. Some time ago I tried to get in touch with poets and to set my views before them, but nothing came of it, and I soon gave the matter up, like a man who means well, but who cannot express his ideas in clear and definite form.   Now I usually confine myself to writing, "I like this," or, "I do not like it." Your poem I like.

As to the story you are writing, — that is a different matter, and I am ready to pass judgment on it to the extent of twenty sheets of paper; if you send it to me and ask me to give you my opinion I shall read it with pleasure. I shall answer you with some definiteness, and shall feel free.

TOLSTOY'S DAUGHTERS

To A. S. Souvorin
Melikhovo.   Oct. 21, 1895.

Tolstoy's daughters are very nice.   They adore their father and have a fanatical faith in him, and that means that Tolstoy really is a great moral force, for if he were insincere and not irreproachable his daughters would be the first to take up a skeptical attitude to him, for daughters are like sparrows: you don't catch them with empty chaff. . . . A man can deceive his fiancée or his mistress as much as he likes, and, in the eyes of a woman he loves, an ass may pass for a philosopher; but a daughter is a different matter. . . .

"THE SEA-GULL"

To A. S. Souvorin
Melikhovo.   Oct. 21, 1895.

Can you imagine it — I am writing a play which I shall probably not finish before the end of November. I am writing it not without pleasure, though I swear fearfully at the conventions of the stage.   It's a comedy, there are three women's parts, six men's, four acts, landscapes (view over a lake); a great deal of conversation about literature, little action, tons of love.

To A. S. Souvorin
Moscow.   Nov. 2, 1895.

My play is progressing, but slowly. I am disturbed in my writing.   Still, I hope to have it done this month.

To E. M. Sh——
Melikhovo.   Nov., 1895.

I have finished my play; the title is "The Sea-Gull." It did not turn out at all as I hoped. Altogether, I am a poor dramatist.

To A. S. Souvorin
Melikhovo.   Nov. 21, 1895.

Well, I have finished with the play. I began it *forte* and ended it *pianissimo* — contrary to all the rules of dramatic art.   It has turned into a novel.   I am rather dissatisfied than satisfied with it, and reading over my new-born play I am more convinced than ever that I am not a dramatist.

The acts are very short. There are four of them. Though it is so far only the skeleton of a play, a plan which will be altered a million times before the coming season, I have ordered two copies to be typed and will send you one; only don't let anyone else read it. . . .

To A. S. Souvorin
Melikhovo.   Dec. 1, 1895.

I did not forget my promise to Anna Ivanovna * to dedicate "The Sea-Gull" to her. It is one of my most unpleasant memories connected with the play. It disgusted me, and its dedication does not tie up with anything in the work, and seems to me absolutely tactless.

To Mikhail Chekhov
Petersburg.   Oct. 15, 1896.

. . . My "Sea-Gull" comes on on the seventeenth of October.   Madame Komissarzhevskaya acts amazingly.

To A. S. Souvorin
Petersburg.   Oct. 18, 1896.

Stop the printing of the play.   I shall never forget yesterday evening, but still I slept well, and am setting off in a very tolerable good humor.   I am not going to produce the play in Moscow. I shall *never* either write plays or have them acted.

To Mikhail Chekhov
Petersburg.   Oct. 18, 1896.

The play has fallen flat, and come down with a crash.

------
* Souvorin's wife.

There was an oppressive strained feeling of disgrace and bewilderment in the theatre. The actors played more than stupidly. The moral of it is, one ought not to write plays.

To A. S. Souvorin

Melikhovo. Oct. 22, 1896.

In your last letter (of October 18) you three times call me womanish, and say that I was in a funk. Why this libel? After the performance I had supper at Romanov's. On my word of honor. Then I went to bed, slept soundly, and next day went home without uttering a sound of complaint. If I had been in a funk I should have run from editor to editor and actor to actor, should have nervously entreated them to be considerate, should nervously have inserted useless corrections, and should have spent two or three weeks in Petersburg fussing over my "Sea-Gull," in excitement, in a cold perspiration, in lamentation. . . . When you were with me the night after the performance you told me yourself that it would be the best thing for me to go away; and next morning I got a letter from you to say good-by. How did I show funk? I acted as coldly and reasonably as a man who has made an offer, received a refusal, and has nothing left but to go. Yes, my vanity was stung, but you know it was not a bolt from the blue; I was expecting a failure, and was prepared for it, as I warned you with perfect sincerity beforehand.

When I got home I took a dose of castor oil, and had a cold bath, and now I am ready to write another play. I no longer feel exhausted and irritable, and am not afraid that Davidov and Jean * will come to me and talk about the play. I agree with your corrections, and a thousand thanks for them. Only, please don't regret that you were not at the rehearsals. You know there was in reality only one rehearsal, at which one could make out nothing. One could not see the play at all through the loathsome acting.

I have a telegram from Potapenko — "A colossal success." I have had a letter from Mlle. Veselitsky (Mikulich) whom I don't know. She expresses her sympathy in a tone as if one of my family were dead. It's really quite inappropriate; that's all nonsense, though.

To N. I. Korobov
Melikhovo. Nov. 1, 1896.

My play came off with much noise, in the sense that they criticise it as meaningless and scold me so that the heavens grow hot; others again, assert that it is a "marvelous" play. I can't make it out. I fled from Petersburg in all haste, and I am now receiving many letters and even telegrams; the mail-boxes are full to overflowing.

To A. F. Koni
Melikhovo. Nov. 11, 1896.

You cannot imagine how your letter rejoiced me. I saw from the front only the first two acts of my play. Afterwards I sat behind the scenes and felt the whole time that "The Sea-Gull" was a failure. After the performance that night and next day, I was assured that I had hatched out nothing but idiots, that my play was clumsy from the stage

---

* Shcheglov.

point of view, that it was not clever, that it was unintelligible, even senseless, and so on and so on. You can imagine my position — it was a collapse such as I had never dreamed of! I felt ashamed and vexed, and I went away from Petersburg full of doubts of all sorts. I thought that if I had written and put on the stage a play so obviously brimming over with monstrous defects, I had lost all instinct and that, therefore, my machinery must have gone wrong for good. After I had reached home, they wrote to me from Petersburg that the second and third performances were a success; several letters, some signed, some anonymous, came, praising the play and abusing the critics. I read them with pleasure, but still I felt vexed and ashamed, and the idea forced itself upon me that if kind-hearted people thought it was necessary to comfort me, it meant that I was in a bad way. But your letter has acted upon me in a most definite way. I have known you a long time, I have a deep respect for you, and I believe in you more than in all the critics taken together — you felt that when you write your letter, and that is why it is so excellent and convincing. My mind is at rest now, and I can think of the play and the performance without loathing. Komissarzhevskaya is a wonderful actress. At one of the rehearsals many people were moved to tears as they looked at her, and said that she was the first actress in Russia to-day; but at the first performance she was affected by the general attitude of hostility to my "Sea-Gull," and was, as it were, intimidated by it and lost her voice. Our press takes a cold tone to her that doesn't do justice to her merits, and I am sorry for her. Allow me to thank you with all my heart for your letter. Believe me, I value the feelings that prompted you to write it far more than I can express in words, and the sympathy you call "unnecessary" at the end of your letter I shall never forget, whatever happens.

To Vl. I. Nemirovich-Danchenko
Melikhovo. Nov. 20, 1896.

Yes, my "Sea-Gull" was a decided failure in Petersburg at the first performance. The theatre was full of anger, the air tense with contempt. And I, — following the laws of physics — bolted from Petersburg like a bomb. You and Sumbatov are to blame for this, as you incited me to write the play.

PROFESSIONAL ISOLATION

To V. I. Nemirovich-Danchenko
Melikhovo. Nov. 26, 1896.

I am answering the chief substance of your letter — the question why we so rarely talk of serious subjects. When people are silent, it is because they have nothing to talk about or because they are ill at ease. What is there to talk about? We have no politics, we have neither public life nor club life, or even a life of the streets; our civic existence is poor, monotonous, burdensome, and uninteresting — and to talk is as boring as corresponding with L. You say that we are literary men, and that of itself makes our life a rich one. Is that so? We are stuck in our profession up to our ears, it has gradually isolated us from the

external world, and the upshot of it is that we have little
free time, little money, few books, we read little and re-
luctantly, we hear little, we rarely go anywhere. Should
we talk about literature? . . . Every year it's the same
thing again and again, and all we usually say about literature may be reduced to discussing who write better, and
who write worse. Conversations upon wider and more
general topics never catch on, because when you have
tundras and Esquimaux all around you, general ideas, being so inappropriate to the reality, quickly lose shape and
slip away like thoughts of eternal bliss. Are we to talk of
personal life? Yes, that may sometimes be interesting and
we might perhaps talk about it; but there again we are
constrained, we are reserved and insincere: we are re-
strained by an instinct of self-preservation and we are
afraid. We are afraid of being overheard by some uncultured Esquimau who does not like us, and whom we
don't like either. I personally am afraid that my acquaintance, N., whose cleverness attracts us, will hold
forth with raised finger, in every railway carriage and
every house, about me, settling the question why I became
so intimate with X. while I was beloved by Z. I am afraid
of our morals, I am afraid of our ladies. . . . In short, for
our silence, for the frivolity and dullness of our conversations, don't blame yourself or me, blame the climate, the
vast distances, what you will, and let circumstances go on
their own fateful, relentless course, hoping for a better
future.

WRITING FROM MEMORY

To F. D. Batiushkov
Nice. Dec. 15, 1897.

I am writing a story for *The Cosmopolis*. I write slowly, a bit at a time, at odd moments. I usually write slowly, with effort, but here, in this room, at a strange table, in fine weather when one wants to be out of doors, it is still worse; and so I cannot promise you a story in less than two weeks.

In one of your letters you expressed a desire that I should send you an international story, taking for my subject something from the life here. Such a story I can write only in Russia from reminiscences. I can only write from reminiscences, and I have never written direct from Nature. I have let my memory sift the subject, so that only what is important or typical is left in it as in a filter. . . .

ZOLA AND THE DREYFUS CASE

To F. D. Batiushkov
Nice. Jan. 28, 1898.

. . . We talk of nothing here but Zola and Dreyfus. The immense majority of educated people are on Zola's side and believe that Dreyfus is innocent. Zola has gained immensely in public esteem; his letters of protest are like a breath of fresh air, and every Frenchman has felt that, thank God! there is still justice in the world, and that if an innocent man is condemned there is still someone to champion him. The French papers are worthless. *Novoe Vremya* is simply loathsome. . . .

To A. A. Khotyaïntseva
Nice. Feb., 1898.

You want to know whether I still think that Zola is right. I ask you: do you think so ill of me to imagine for one moment that I am not on Zola's side? I would not exchange one of his fingernails for all of those who are sitting on his case at the court, all those generals and high-born witnesses. I am reading the stenographic record and I don't see how Zola can be in the wrong, and why all those "preuves" are necessary.

To A. S. Souvorin
Nice. Feb. 6, 1898.

. . . You write that you are annoyed with Zola, and here everyone has a feeling as though a new, better Zola had arisen. In his trial he has been cleansed as though in turpentine from grease-spots, and now shines before the French in his true brilliance. There is a purity and moral elevation that was not suspected in him. You should follow the whole scandal from the very beginning. The degradation of Dreyfus, whether it was just or not, made on all (you were of the number I remember) a painful and depressing impression. It was noticed that at the time of the sentence Dreyfus behaved like a decent, well-disciplined officer, while those present at the sentence, the journalists for instance, shouted at him, "Hold your tongue, Judas," — that is, behaved badly and indecently. Everyone came back

from the sentence dissatisfied and with a troubled conscience. Dreyfus's counsel, Démange, an honest man, who
even during the preliminary stages of the trial felt that
something shifty was being done behind the scenes, was
particularly dissatisfied — and then the experts who, to con-
vince themselves that they had not made a mistake, kept
talking of nothing but Dreyfus, of his being guilty, and
kept wandering all over Paris! . . .

Of the experts one turned out to be mad, the author of
a monstrously absurd project; two were eccentric creatures.

People could not help talking of the Intelligence Department at the War Office, that military consistory which
is employed in hunting for spies and reading other people's
letters; it began to be said that the head of that Department, Sandherr, was suffering from progressive paralysis;
Paty de Clam has shown himself to be something after the
style of Tausch of Berlin; Picquart suddenly took his departure mysteriously, causing a lot of talk. All at once a
series of gross judicial blunders came to light. By degrees
people became convinced that Dreyfus had been condemned on the strength of a secret document, which had
been shown neither to the accused man nor to his de-
fending counsel, and decent, law-abiding people saw in
this a fundamental breach of justice. If the letter were the
work not simply of Wilhelm, but of the center of the solar
system, it ought to have been shown to Démange. All
sorts of guesses were made as to the contents of this letter,
the most impossible stories circulated. Dreyfus was an
officer, the military were suspect; Dreyfus was a Jew, the
Jews were suspect. People began talking about militarism,

about the Jews.   Such utterly disreputable people as
Drumont held up their heads; little by little they stirred up
a regular pother on a substratum of anti-semitism, on a
substratum that smelt of the shambles. When something
is wrong with us we look for the causes outside ourselves,
and readily find them. "It's the Frenchman's nastiness,
it's the Jews', it's Wilhelm's."   Capital, brimstone, the
free-masons, the Syndicate, the Jesuits — they are all
bogeys, but how they relieve our uneasiness!   They are,
of course, a bad sign.   Since the French have begun talking about the Jews, about the Syndicate, it shows they are
feeling uncomfortable, that there is a worm gnawing at
them, that they feel the need of these bogeys to soothe their
over-excited conscience.

Then this Esterhazy, a duelist in the style of Turgeniev's duelists, an insolent ruffian, who had long been an
object of suspicion, and was not respected by his comrades; the striking resemblance of his handwriting with
that of the bordereau, the Uhlan's letters, his threats
which for some reason he does not carry out; finally the
judgment, utterly mysterious, strangely deciding that the
bordereau was written in Esterhazy's handwriting but not
his hand! . . . And the gas has been continually accumu-
lating, there has come to be a feeling of acute tension, of
overwhelming oppression. The fighting in the court was
a purely nervous manifestation, simply, the hysterical result of that tension, and Zola's letter and his trial are a
manifestation of the same kind. What would you have?
The best people, always in advance of the nation, were
bound to be the first to raise an agitation — and so it has

been. The first to speak was Scheurer-Kestner, of whom Frenchmen who know him intimately (according to Kovalevsky) say that he is a "sword-blade," so spotless and without blemish is he. The second is Zola, and now he is being tried.

Yes, Zola is not Voltaire, and we are none of us Voltaires, but there are in life conjunctions of circumstances when the reproach that we are not Voltaires is least of all appropriate. Think of Korolenko, who defended the Multanovsky natives and saved them from penal servitude. Dr. Haas is not a Voltaire either, and yet his wonderful life has been well spent up to the end.

I am well acquainted with the case from the stenographers' report, which is utterly different from what is in the newspapers, and I have a clear view of Zola. The chief point is that he is sincere — that is, he bases his judgments simply on what he sees, and not on phantoms, like the others. And sincere people can be mistaken, no doubt of it, but such mistakes do less harm than calculated insincerity, prejudgments, or political considerations. Let Dreyfus be guilty, and Zola is still right, since it is the duty of writers not to accuse, not to prosecute, but to champion even the guilty once they have been condemned and are enduring punishment. I shall be told: "What of the political position? The interest of the State?" But great writers and artists ought to take part in politics only so far as they have to protect themselves from politics. There are plenty of accusers, prosecutors, and gendarmes without them, and in any case, the rôle of Paul suits them better than that of Saul. Whatever the verdict may be, Zola will anyway experience a vivid delight after the trial, his old age will be a fine old age, and he will die with a conscience at peace, or at any rate greatly solaced. The French are very sick. They clutch at every word of comfort and at every genuine reproach coming to them from outside. That is why Bernstein's letter and our Zakrevsky's article (which was read here in the *Novosti**) have had such a great success here, and why they are so disgusted by the abuse of Zola, such as the gutter press, which they despise, flings at him every day. However neurotic Zola may be, still he stands before the court of French common sense, and the French love him for it and are proud of him, even though they do applaud the Generals who, in the simplicity of their hearts, scare them first with the honor of the army, then with war. . . .

ZOLA

To G. M. Chekhov
Nice.   February 22, 1898.

You ask my opinion regarding Zola and his trial. First of all, I judge from the evidence: on Zola's side is all the European intelligentsia, and against him all that is bad and dubious. The affair stands thus: imagine that the university authorities, by mistake, expelled one student instead of another; you begin to protest, and they shout at you: "You are attacking science!" — though all that the university chancellor has in common with science is that

---

* *Novosti Dnya—Daily News.*

the functionary and the professor both wear blue coats; you continue to plead, present assurances, evidence, — their cry is: "Conviction!" "Please," you say, "let us go to the chancellor's office and examine the books." — "You must not! That is the chancellor's secret! . . ." There it is. The psychology of the French government is clear. It is like a good woman who, having deceived her husband once, afterwards commits a series of vulgar errors, falls a victim to blackmail, and finally kills herself, — and all to hide her first mistakes, — in the same way the French government is now marching to its downfall, shutting its eyes, veering to right and left, — only not to acknowledge itself in the wrong.

The *Novoe Vremya* is conducting a senseless campaign; on the other hand, most Russian newspapers, if they are not for Zola, are opposed to his trial. Cassation will lead to nothing, even with a favorable issue. The question will decide itself somehow, eventually, following upon the explosion of all the steam that is gathering in the Frenchmen's heads.   Murder will out.

THE LITERARY ENTOURAGE

To L. A. Avilov

Melikhovo.   July 25, 1898.

I am disgusted with writing and I do not know what to do.   I'd take up medicine with pleasure; I would look for a post, but I haven't the physical flexibility. When I write, or think about writing, I experience an aversion, — as if I were eating sour-cabbage soup from which a roach had just been removed, — forgive the comparison. It is not writing itself toward which I feel this aversion, — it is really toward the literary "entourage" which one cannot escape, and which one always carries along as the earth carries its atmosphere.

THE MOSCOW ART THEATRE

To A. S. Souvorin
Yalta. Oct. 8, 1898.

I read in the *Novoe Vremya* a remark about the theatre of Nemirovich and Stanislavsky, and about" Feodor Ivanovich," and I did not quite understand its psychology. You were fond of the theatre, and were so heartily welcomed there, that the origin of the statement in the newspaper must have been some complicated misunderstanding that I know nothing about. What has happened? By the way, I attended the rehearsal of "Feodor Ivanovich" before my departure. I was agreeably touched by the intelligence that marked the production; real art was on the stage, though only second-class talents were performing. Irena, I think, is excellent. The voice, elevation of character, her sincerity, are so masterful that I enjoy the mere recollection of it all. Feodor seemed to me rather poor. Gordunov and Shusky are good, and the old peasant is excellent. But the best of all is Irena. If I were to stay in Moscow, I'd fall in love with that Irena.*

---
* The rôle of Irena was performed by Mme. Olga Knipper who later married Chekhov.

To V. E. Meierhold.†

Dear Vsevolod Emilevich, I have not at hand a copy of the text of Johannes' part, and hence I can speak only in general terms. If you will send me the part, I shall read it through, refresh my memory, and give you the details. For the present I shall call your attention to a few things that may be of practical interest to you.

First of all, Johannes is very intelligent; he is a young scientist brought up in a university town. He lacks completely the elements of the bourgeois. He is a well-bred man, accustomed to the society of respectable people (like Anna); in his movements and appearance he is the tender and immature man reared in the bosom of a loving family and still his mother's pet. Johannes is a German scientist; he is, therefore, steady in his relations with men. On the other hand, he is as tender as a woman when in the company of women. As a typical illustration of these traits, there is the scene with his wife, in which he cannot help being tender toward her in spite of the fact that he already loves, or is beginning to love, Anna. Now as to the nervousness. One must not underline this nervous temperament, because the highly strung, neuropathological nature would hide and misrepresent the much more important loneliness, — the loneliness experienced only by fine, and at the same time healthy (in the fullest sense of the word) organisms. Depict a lonely man, and represent him as nervous only to the extent indicated by the text.

---

† The letter refers to the performance of Hauptmann's *Lonely Lives*, by the Moscow Art Theatre. Meierhold p'ayed the part of Johannes. The letter is found in the *Yearbook of the Imperial Theatres*, for 1909, No. 5.

Do not treat this nervousness as a separate phenomenon. Remember that in our day every cultured man, even the most healthy, is most irritable in his own home and among his own family, because the discord between the present and the past is first of all apparent in the family. It is an irritability which is chronic, which has no pathos, and does not end in catastrophic consequences; it is an irritability that guests cannot perceive, and which, in its fullest force, is experienced first by the nearest relatives, the wife, the mother. It is, so to say, an intimate, family irritation and nervousness. Do not spend much time on it; present it only as *one* of many typical traits; do not stress it, — or you will appear, not a lonely young man, but an irritable one. I know that Konstantin Sergeyevich * will insist on this superfluous nervousness; he exaggerates it, — but, do not yield; do not sacrifice the beauty and power of the voice for the sake of such a detail as the accent. Do not make the sacrifice, because in this case the irritation is only a detail.

ABOUT MAXIM GORKY

To A. M. Pieshkov (Maxim Gorky)
Yalta. Dec. 3, 1898.

You ask for my opinion of your stories. My opinion? An unquestionable talent, and a real, a great talent at that. In the story "On the Steppe," for instance, there is so much power that I even became envious that I was not its

* Stanislavsky.

author. You are an artist, a clear-eyed man; you feel keenly, you are plastic, i.e., when you picture a thing you see it, and feel it with your hand. This is real art. Now you have my opinion, and I am very glad that I can express it to you. I am very glad, I repeat, and if we were to meet and speak for an hour or two, you would see how highly I value you and what hopes I have in your talent.

Shall I now speak of your defects? This is not so easy. To speak of the defects of a man of talent is the same as to speak of the defects of a big tree that grows in a garden; the main reality here is not in the tree but in the emotion aroused in him who looks at the tree. Isn't it so?

I shall begin by saying that you, in my opinion, have no self-restraint. You are like a spectator in a theatre who expresses his delight so unreservedly that it prevents himself and others from listening. This lack of self-restraint is especially evident in the descriptions of nature with which you interrupt the dialogue; as one reads these descriptions one wishes that they were more compact, shorter, say about two or three lines or so. The frequent mention of "softness," "whisper," "velvety smoothness," etc., impart to these descriptions a certain floridness, monotony, — they cool one's ardor and almost tire one. The lack of self-restraint is felt also in the portrayal of women ("Malva"; "On the Raft"), and of love scenes. It is not a free swing, a broadness of the brush, but precisely the lack of self-restraint. Then, too, there is a frequent use of words entirely out of place in stories of your type. "Accompaniment," "disc," "harmony" — such words are disturbing. In the delineation of the intelligentsia there is something forced, as if you feel a sense of uncertainty. This is not due to lack of study of the intelligentsia; you know them, but it seems as if you do not know from what angle to approach them.

How old are you? I do not know you. I don't know where you come from and who you are, but it seems to me that, while you are still young, you ought to leave Nizhni and for two or three years to live among, to rub elbows, as it were, with literary people and literature. Not in order to learn a different tune or to acquire more cunning or skill, but in order to plunge over head and ears in literature and learn to love it. Besides, the provinces make one prematurely old. Potapenko, Mamin, Ertel, — they are all excellent people. At first, perhaps, you will feel a sense of tedium in their company, but a year or two later you will grow accustomed to them, and they will repay you with interest for the unpleasantness and the discomforts of town-life.

Be well and happy. I warmly press your hand. Once more, thanks for your letter.

To Maxim Gorky

Yalta. Jan. 3, 1899.

. . . Apparently you have misunderstood me a little. I did not write to you of coarseness of style, but only of the incongruity of foreign, not genuinely Russian, or rarely used words. In other authors such words as, for instance, "fatalistically," pass unnoticed, but your things are musical, harmonious, and every crude touch jars fearfully. Of course it is a question of taste, and perhaps this is only a sign of excessive fastidiousness in me, or the conservatism of a man who has adopted definite habits for himself long ago. I am resigned to *"a collegiate assessor,"* and *"a captain* of the second *rank,"* in descriptions, but *"flirt"* and *"champion"* when they occur in descriptions excite repulsion in me.

Are you self-educated?   In your stories you are completely an artist and at the same time an "educated" man in the truest sense.

Nothing is less characteristic of you than coarseness; you are clever and subtle and delicate in your feelings. Your best things are "On the Steppe," and "On the Raft," — did I write to you about that? They are splendid things, masterpieces; they show the artist who has passed through a very good school. I don't think that I am mistaken. The only defect is the lack of restraint, the lack of grace. When a man spends the least possible number of movements over some definite action, that is grace.   One is conscious of superfluity in your expenditure.

The descriptions of nature are the work of an artist; you are a real landscape painter. Only the frequent personification (anthropomorphism) when the sea breathes, the sky gazes, the steppe barks, nature whispers, speaks, mourns, and so on — such metaphors make your descriptions somewhat monotonous, sometimes sweetish, sometimes not clear; beauty and expressiveness in nature are attained only by simplicity, by such simple phrases as "The sun set," "It was dark," "It began to rain," and so on — and that simplicity is characteristic of you in the highest degree, more so perhaps than of any other writer. . . .

I do not care for the first number of the revived *Zhizn.* It is not serious. N.'s story is naïve and false; N. M.'s story is a crude imitation of something, of its forebear, Orlov, — but crude and also naïve. You won't get far with stories of this kind. In your own "Kirillkys" * the general effect is weakened by the figure of the provincial official, though the tone is maintained throughout. Never portray provincial officials.   Nothing is so easy as to describe an irritating official; a certain class of readers likes it, but it is the most unpleasant class, the most untalented. To a figure of a newly created type, like the provincial official, I experience the same aversion as I do to the "flirt," — so I may not be right. But I live in the country; I am acquainted with rural officials and those of the neighboring districts, — I have known them a long time, and I find that neither their characters nor their activities are at all typical; they are altogether uninteresting, — and there, I think, I am right.

Now about vagabondage.   It is a very fine, alluring thing; but with the years you somehow get heavy, and prefer to remain fixed in the one place. And the literary profession begins to draw you. Through failure and disillusionment there quickly comes a time when you no longer see life in its reality, — and the past, when I was so free, seems to me no longer my own, but another's.

To A. S. Souvorin
Yalta.   Jan. 27, 1899.
Have you read the author, Gorky? An undoubted talent.

----

* *That Cyril—*a story.

If you have not read him, get his collected works, and for your first acquaintance with him read the two stories, "On the Raft" and "On the Steppe." The latter story is a model, — an ace, as Stasov says.

To L. A. Avilov
Yalta. Feb. 26, 1899.

You like Gorky? I think that Gorky is a genuine talent; his brushes and colors are real; his talent is sustained, daring. His "On the Steppe" is a wonderful work.

To Maxim Gorky
Moscow. June 22, 1899.

Why are you still so blue, dear Alexei Maximovich? Why do you so furiously revile your "Foma Gordyeev"? With your permission, here are, besides others, two reasons. You began with success, began noisily, — and now it all presents itself to you as ordinary and commonplace, leaves you unsatisfied, and wearies you. That is the first cause. Secondly, a litterateur cannot with impunity live in the provinces. Whatever you may say, you have tasted literature, you are already hopelessly poisoned, you are a writer and a writer you will remain. As a natural thing the condition of a litterateur is to keep close always to the literary sphere, to live near writers, to breathe literature. Do not fight against Nature therefore; become its subject once for all, — and go to Petersburg or Moscow. Abuse the litterateurs, refuse to recognize them, condemn half of them, but live among them.

To Maxim Gorky
Moscow. June 27, 1899.

When I wrote that you began noisily and with éclat, I had not the slightest notion of a malicious meaning, nor did I intend to be sharp. I merely wanted to say that you had not been to the literary college, but began direct from the academy, and now it has become dull for you to serve without singers. I wish to say: wait a year or two; you will get yourself in hand, and will see that your dearest "Foma Gordyeev" is really in no way to blame.

You are planning to tour Russia on foot? Pleasant journey! — there is no one to hold you back, although it seems to me that while you are still young and healthy, you ought to travel not on foot, and not third class, but to study at close quarters the public that reads you. And then, in two or three years, you might start out on foot.

To Maxim Gorky
Yalta. Sept. 3, 1899.

First of all, I am against dedications, of whatever it may be, to living people. I used to follow the fashion in dedications, and now feel, if you please, that it ought not be done. That is, as a general thing. In the particular case of the dedication to me of "Foma Gordyeev," it gives me great pleasure and honor. Only, how did I merit it? However, it is yours to judge and mine only to thank you and accept. If possible, make the dedication without superfluous words, i.e., write merely, "dedicated to so-and-so," — and it will do. Only Volinsky goes in for long dedications.

Still more of practical advice: print more and not fewer than five or six thousand copies. The book will go quickly. The second edition can be printed together with the first. More advice: when reading the proofs, cross out a host of concrete nouns and other words. You have so many such nouns that the reader's mind finds it a task to concentrate on them, and he soon grows tired. You understand it at once when I say, "The man sat on the grass;" you understand it because it is clear and makes no demands on the attention.   On the other hand, it is not easily understood, and it is difficult for the mind, if I write, "A tall, narrow-chested, middle-sized man, with a red beard, sat on the green grass, already trampled by pedestrians, sat silently, shyly, and timidly looked about him." That is not immediately grasped by the mind, whereas good writing should be grasped at once, — in a second. One thing more: you are by nature lyrical, the *timbre* of your soul is gentle. If you were a composer you would shun the writing of marches. To be rude, noisy, to hurt, to accuse violently, — these things are not natural to your talent.   So you will understand if I advise you not to be sparing when you read the proofs.

ON THE INTELLIGENTSIA

To I. I. Orlov
Yalta.   1899.

. . . I have no faith in our intelligentsia, hypocritical, false, hysterical, ill-bred, lazy; I have no faith in them even when they suffer and complain, for their oppressors come from the same womb as they.   I believe in individuals. I see salvation in a few people living their own private lives, scattered throughout Russia; — whether they be intellectuals or *muzhiks,* the power is in them, though they are few. A man is never a true prophet in his own country; and the individuals of whom I speak play an obscure part in society; they are not domineering, but their work is apparent; whatever comes to pass, science keeps advancing, social self-consciousness increases, moral problems begin to acquire a restless character, etc. And all this is being done despite the procurators, the engineers, the teachers, despite the intelligentsia *en masse,* and despite everything.

"DEAR ACTRESS"

To O. L. Knipper
Yalta. Oct. 4, 1899.

Dear actress, you exaggerate much in your dispirited letter, and this must be true because the newspapers were well disposed toward the first performance. Be that as it may, one or two unsuccessful performances should not be sufficient cause to make you lose courage and pass sleepless nights. Art, and the stage in particular, is a field where one cannot walk without stumbling at times. There are many unsuccessful days and whole seasons of failure ahead of one; and there will be misunderstandings and great disappointments, — one must be prepared for all this; one must expect this, and, in spite of everything, one must doggedly pursue one's path.

To Olga Knipper

Yalta. Nov. 1, 1899.

I understand your mood, dear actress, I understand it very well; but in your place I should not be so desperately upset. Both the part of Anna * and the play itself are not worth wasting so much feeling and nervous energy over. It is already out of date, and there are a great many defects in it; if more than half the performers have not fallen into the right tone, then, of course, it is the fault of the play. That's one thing, and the second is, you must once and for all give up being worried about successes and failures. Don't let that concern you. It's your duty to go on working steadily day by day, altogether quietly, to be prepared for mistakes which are inevitable, for failures — in short, to do your job as actress and let other people count the calls before the curtain. To write or to act, and to be conscious at the time that one is not doing the right thing — that is so usual, and, for beginners, so profitable!

The third thing is that the director has telegraphed that the second performance went magnificently, that everyone played admirably, and that he was completely satisfied.

. . .

THE MOSCOW ART THEATRE

To Vl. I. Nemirovich-Danchenko

Yalta. Nov. 24, 1899.

In your letter there sounds a scarcely audible jarring note, as from an old bell; — it is where you write of the

* In, *Lonely Lives*.

theatre, that you are weary of the pettiness of theatrical life. Oh, do not grow weary, do not cool! The Art Theatre — it constitutes the best pages of that book which will one day be written about the Russian theatre. This theatre is your pride, and the only theatre that I like, although I have never once been it it. If I lived in Moscow, I would try to join your company, were it only in the capacity of doorkeeper, in order to assist at least a little, — and, if possible, to keep you from cooling toward this fine institution.

ON ACTING

To O. L. Knipper
Yalta. Jan. 2, 1900.

I have not congratulated you on the success of "Lonely Lives." I still dream that you will all come to Yalta, that I shall see "Lonely Lives" on the stage, and congratulate you really from my heart. I wrote to Meierhold and urged him in my letter not to be too violent in the part of a nervous man. The immense majority of people are nervous, you know: the greater number suffer, and a small proportion feel acute pain; but where — in streets and in houses — do you see people tearing about, leaping up, and clutching at their heads? Suffering ought to be expressed as it is expressed in life — that is, not by the arms and legs, but by the tone and expression; not by gesticulation, but by grace. Subtle emotions of the soul in educated people must be subtly expressed in an external way. You will say — stage conditions. No conditions allow falsity.

My sister tells me that you played Anna exquisitely. Ah, if only the Art Theatre would come to Yalta. *Novoe Vremya* highly praised your company. There is a change of tactics in that quarter; evidently they are going to praise you all, even in Lent.

GORKY'S STORIES

To Maxim Gorky
Yalta. Jan. 2, 1900.

My story (*i.e.*, "In the Ravine") has already been sent off to *Zhizn*. Did I tell you that I liked your story "An Orphan" extremely, and sent it to Moscow to first-rate readers? There is a certain Professor A. B. Fokht in the Medical Faculty in Moscow who reads Slyeptsov capitally. I don't know a better reader. So I have sent your "Orphan" to him. Did I tell you how much I liked a story in your third volume, "My Traveling Companion"? There is the same strength in it as in "On the Steppe." If I were you, I would take the best things out of your three volumes and republish them in one volume at a rouble — and that would be something really remarkable for vigor and harmony. As it is, everything seems shaken up together in the three volumes; there are no weak things, but it leaves an impression as though the three volumes were not the work of one author but of seven.

To A. S. Souvorin
Yalta. Jan. 23, 1900.

As regards the Academy, you have not sufficiently informed yourself. Writers will *not* be real academicians.

The artist-writers will make honorary academicians *ober*-academicians, arch-academicians, but merely academicians, — never, or not soon. They will never invite into their ark people whom they do not know and do not trust. Tell me: why was it necessary to devise the rank of honorary academician?

However that may be, I am glad they elected me. Now they will write on my foreign passport that I am an Academician. And the Moscow doctors were glad. It came to me from the clouds.

ELECTION TO THE ACADEMY

To Alex. P. Chekhov
Yalta.   Jan. 25, 1900.

News of the election to the Academy came when I was not well, — and all the charm was lost, as I was indifferent to everything.

ADVICE TO GORKY

To Maxim Gorky
Yalta.   Feb. 3, 1900.

Thank you for your letter, for the lines about Tolstoy and about "Uncle Vanya," which I haven't seen on the stage; thanks altogether for not forgetting me. Here in this blessed Yalta one could hardly keep alive without letters. . . .

You have pleurisy. If so, why do you stay on in Nizhni. Why? What do you want with that Nizhni, by the way?

What glue keeps you sticking to that town? If you like Moscow, as you write, why don't you live in Moscow? In Moscow there are theatres and all the rest of it, and, what matters most of all, Moscow is handy for going abroad; while living in Nizhni you'll stick in Nizhni, and never go farther than Vasilsursk. You want to see more, to know more, to have a wider range. Your imagination is quick to seize and hold, but it is like a big oven which is not provided with fuel enough. One feels this in general, and in particular in the stories: you present two or three figures in a story, but these figures stand apart, outside the mass; one sees that these figures are living in your imagination, but only these figures — the mass is not grasped. I except from this criticism your Crimean things (for instance, "My Traveling Companion"), in which, besides the figures, there is a feeling of the human mass out of which they have come, and atmosphere and background — everything, in fact. See what a lecture I am giving you — and all that you may not go on staying in Nizhni. You are a young man, strong and tough; if I were you I should make a tour in India and all sorts of places. I would take my degree in two or more faculties — I would, yes, I would! You laugh, but I do feel so badly treated at being forty already, at having asthma and all sorts of miserable things which prevent my living freely. Anyway, be a good fellow and a good comrade, and don't be angry with me for preaching at you like a bishop.

Write to me. I look forward to "Foma Gordyeev," which I haven't yet read properly.

BOREDOM

To Maxim Gorky
Yalta. Feb. 15, 1900.

I am bored, not in the sense of *weltschmerz*, not in the sense of being weary of existence, but simply bored from want of people, from want of music which I love, and from want of women, of whom there are none in Yalta. I am bored without caviare and pickled cabbage.

Yes, I have the right now to insist on the fact that I am forty, that I am a man no longer young. I used to be the youngest literary man, but you have appeared on the scene and I became more dignified at once, and no one calls me the youngest now.

PROTEST TO THE ACADEMY

To The President of the Academy *
Yalta. Aug. 25, 1902.

In December of last year I received the news of the election of A. M. Pieshkov † to the Academy, and I at once went to see A. M. Pieshkov, who was then in the Crimea. I was the first to bring him the news of his election, and to congratulate him. Shortly thereafter it was revealed in the newspapers that in view of the fact that Pieshkov had been tried in court under the 1035th Statute, the election was not confirmed. It was also indi-

---

* Konstantin Konstantinovich, Grand Duke of Russia.
† Maxim Gorky.

cated specifically that this announcement came from the Academy of Science, and since I am an Honorary Academician, the notice emanated in part from me. I congratulated him heartily, and also declared the election annulled, — such a contradiction is beyond my understanding. I was unable to reconcile my conscience to it, and after long consideration I could come to only one decision, exceedingly unpleasant and sad for me, — namely, respectfully to request your Imperial Highness for the suspension of my status as Honorary Academician.

REALISM IN LITERATURE

To S. P. Diagilev
Yalta. Dec. 30, 1902.

. . . You write that we talked of a serious religious movement in Russia. We talked of a movement not in Russia but in the intellectual class. I won't say anything about Russia; the intellectuals so far are only playing at religion, and for the most part from having nothing to do. One may say of the cultured part of our public that it has moved away from religion, and is moving further and further away from it, whatever people may say and however many philosophical and religious societies may be formed. Whether it is a good or a bad thing I cannot undertake to decide; I will only say that the religious movement of which you write is one thing, and the whole trend of modern culture is another, and one cannot place the second in any casual connection with the first. Modern culture is only the first beginning of work for a great future work which will perhaps go on for tens of thousands of years, in order that man may, if only in the remote future, come to know the truth of the real God — that is not, I conjecture, by seeking in Dostoevsky, but by clear knowledge, as one knows twice two are four. Modern culture is the first beginning of the work, while the religious movement of which we talked is a survival, almost the end of what has ceased, or is ceasing to exist. But it is a long story; one can't put it all into a letter. . . .

"THE CHERRY ORCHARD"

To V. F. Komissarzhevskaya
Yalta. Jan. 27, 1903.

This much about the play:

(1) The play is already in my mind, it is true, and the title chosen ("The Cherry Orchard," — but this is a secret), and I shall start on it not later than the end of February, providing of course, I am well.

(2) In this play the central person is a woman along in years, to the great regret of the author.

(3) Should I turn it over to the Art Theatre, then according to existing rules and regulations of the theatre the play is given over to the sole disposal of the Art Theatre in Moscow and Petersburg, — and I can in no way help this. If the Art Theatre does not travel to Petersburg in 1904 (which is altogether possible), I shall assign the play to you without further ado, providing it is suitable for your theatre. Or, here is something else: why not a play for you? Not for this or the other theatre,

but for you.   This has been a long-cherished desire of mine. . . .

You write: "I have in me such faith that, should it break, it would kill me. . . ." etc. Right, you are right, but, for Heaven's sake, do not place all this faith on the new theatre. You are an artist, and that is like being a good sailor: no matter on what ship he sails, be it a government vessel or a merchant ship, he remains under all circumstances a good sailor.

To K. S. Stanislavsky
Yalta. July 28, 1903.

My play "The Cherry Orchard" is not yet finished; it makes slow progress, which I put down to laziness, fine weather, and the difficulty of the subject. . . .

I think your part is all right, though I can't undertake to decide, as I can judge very little of a play by reading it. . . .

To Vl. I. Nemirovich-Danchenko
Yalta. August 22, 1903.

Now as to my play, "The Cherry Orchard," — so far I am making good progress. I work on it each day, but not too hard, and if I am a bit late in completing it, it would make little difference. I reduced the stage-set to a minimum; no special decorations will be required.

In the second act I substituted for the river an old chapel and a well. This is better. But in the second act you will make provision for a real green field, and a path, and an horizon wider than is usual on the stage.

To Vl. I. Nemirovich-Danchenko
Yalta. Sept. 2, 1903.

My play (if I continue to make as much headway as up to the present) will be completed very soon; don't worry. The second act presented many difficulties, but I seem to have overcome them. I shall call the play a comedy.

To Madame Stanislavsky
Yalta. Sept. 15, 1903

. . . Don't believe anybody — no living soul has read my play yet; I have written for you not the part of a "canting hypocrite," but of a very nice girl, with which you will, I hope, be satisfied. I have almost finished the play, but eight or ten days ago I was taken ill with coughing and weakness — in fact, last year's business over again. Now — that is to-day — it is warmer and I feel better, but still I cannot write, as my head is aching. Olga * will not bring the play; I will send the four acts together as soon as it is possible for me to set to work for a whole day. It has turned out not a drama, but a comedy, in parts a farce, indeed, and I am afraid I shall catch it from Vladimir Ivanich. . . . †

I can't come for the opening of your season, I must stay in Yalta till November. Olga, who has grown fatter and stronger in the summer, will probably come to Moscow on Sunday. I shall remain alone, and of course shall take advantage of that. As a writer it is essential for me to

------

* Mme. Knipper-Chekhova.
† Nemirovich-Danchenko.

observe women, to study them, and so, I regret to say, I cannot be a faithful husband. As I observe women chiefly for the sake of my plays, in my opinion the Art Theatre ought to increase my wife's salary or give her a pension! . . .

To K. S. Stanislavsky

Yalta. Oct. 30, 1903.

When I was writing Lopakhin, I thought of it as a part for you. If for any reason you don't care for it, take the part of Gaev. Lopakhin is a merchant, of course, but he is a very decent person in every sense. He must behave with perfect decorum, like an educated man, with no petty ways or tricks of any sort, and it seemed to me this part, the central one of the play, would come out brilliantly in your hands. . . . In choosing an actor for the part you must remember that Varya, a serious and religious girl, is in love with Lopakhin; she wouldn't be in love with a mere money-grubber. . . .

To Vl. I. Nemirovich-Danchenko

Yalta. Nov. 2, 1903.

And now about the play.

(1) Anya can be played by anybody convenient, even by an altogether unknown actress, — only she must be young and look young, and her voice must be youthful and ringing. This is not one of the important rôles.

(2) Varya is a more serious part, if Marya Petrovna * takes it. Without Marya Petrovna it will be a little insipid

---

* Mme. Stanislavsky.

and crude, and will have to be changed, softened. M. P. cannot repeat herself, first, because she is talented, and second, because Varya does not resemble Sonya and Natasha; she is a figure in a black dress, a bit nun-like, a bit stupid, somewhat tearful, etc., etc.

(3) Gaev and Lopakhin — let these rôles be left to Konst. Serg,* to try to make his choice. If he were to take Lopakhin and the rôle pleased him, then the play would be successful. But if Lopakhin is poorly played by a second-rate actor, both the rôle and the play will fail.

(4) Pishchik — Gribunin. God keep N. from this rôle.

(5) Charlotte — a question mark . . . of course, you must not give it away; Muratova will perhaps be good, but not comical. For this rôle Mme. Knipper.

(6) Epikhodov — if Moskvin wants it, let him have it. He will be an excellent Epikhodov. I supposed that Luzhsky was to play it.

(7) Firs — Artyom.

(8) Dunyasha — Khalutina.

(9) Yasha. If Alexandrov, of whom you write, is the one who is your assistant-manager, let him have Yasha. Moskvin would make a wonderful Yasha. And I should not object to Leonidov for the part.

(10) The Tramp — Gromov.

(11) The station-master, the one who reads "The Transgressor" in the third act, — an actor who has a bass voice.

---

* Stanislavsky.

Charlotte does not speak in a hybrid way, but uses the pure Russian tongue; but, on rare occasions, she pronounces the soft ending of a word, hard, and she confuses the masculine and feminine genders of adjectives. Pishchik is a Russian, an old man, worn out by the gout, age, and satiety; stout, dressed in a sleeveless undercoat (à la Simov),* boots without heels. Lopakhin — a white waistcoat, yellow shoes; when walking, swings his arms, a broad stride, thinks deeply while walking, walks as if on a straight line. Hair not short, and therefore often throws back his head; while in thought he passes his hand through his beard, combing it from the back forward, i.e., from the neck toward the mouth. Trofimov, I think, is clear. Varya — black dress, wide belt.

Three years I spent writing "The Cherry Orchard," and for three years I have been telling you that it is necessary to invite an actress for the rôle of Liubov Andreevna. And now you see you are trying to solve a puzzle that won't work out.

To K. S. Alekseyev (Stanislavsky)
Yalta. Nov. 5, 1903.

The house in the play is two-storied, a large one. But in the third act does it not speak of a stairway leading down? Nevertheless, this third act worries me. . . . N. has it that the third act takes place in "some kind of hotel;" . . . evidently I made an error in the play. The action does not pass in "some kind of hotel," but in a *drawing-*

---

* Actor, Moscow Art Theatre.

room. If I mention an hotel in the play, which I cannot now doubt, after Vl. Iv.'s * letter, please telegraph me. We must correct it; we cannot issue it thus, with grave errors distorting its meaning.

The house must be large, solid; wooden (like Aksakov's, which, I think, S. T. Morozov has seen) or stone, it is all the same. It is very old and imposing; country-residents do not take such houses; such houses are usually wrecked and the material employed for the construction of a country-house. The furniture is ancient, stylish, solid; ruin and debt have not affected the surroundings.

When they buy such a house, they reason thus: it is cheaper and easier to build a new and smaller one than to repair this old one.

Your shepherd played well. That was most essential.

To K. S. Stanislavsky
Yalta.   Nov. 10, 1903.

Of course the scenery for III. and IV. can be the same, the hall and the staircase. Please do just as you like about the scenery, I leave it entirely to you; I am amazed and generally sit with my mouth wide open at your theatre. There can be no question about it, whatever you do will be excellent, a hundred times better than anything I could invent. . . .

To K. S. Alekseyev (Stanislavsky)
Yalta.   Nov. 23, 1903.

Hay-mowing time is usually from the 20-22 of June; by

---

* Nemirovich-Danchenko.

that time the rail-birds have become still, and the frogs, too. It is not a graveyard now; long ago there was a cemetery on the spot. Two or three scattered slabs of sandstone are all that remains. The bridge is very good. If one can present the train without noise, without the least sound, then go ahead. I do not oppose the plan of the single setting for Acts III. and IV.; only, in Act IV. the exits and entrances must be natural.

To V. F. Komissarzhevskaya
Moscow. Jan. 6, 1904.

I write you this with a light heart, because of my deep conviction that "The Cherry Orchard" is not for you. The central figure in the play is a woman, an old woman, wholly of the past, with nothing in her of the present; the other rôles, at least the women, are trivial and uninteresting, not in the least suited for you.

To F. D. Batiushkov
Moscow. Jan. 19, 1904.

. . . At the first performance of "The Cherry Orchard" on the 17th of January, they gave me an ovation, so lavish, warm, and really so unexpected, that I can't get over it even now. . . .

A MOSCOW HAMLET

1891

A MOSCOW HAMLET

1891

I am a Moscow Hamlet. Yes. In Moscow I visit the houses, the theatres, the restaurants, and the editors' offices, and everywhere I say exactly the same thing: "God, what boredom! What oppressive boredom!" And they answer me sympathetically, "Yes, truly, terribly boring."

This goes on night and day. And at night, when back in my home, I lie down to sleep and in the darkness ask myself why, after all, I am so painfully bored, something heavy turns in my breast — and I recall how a week ago, in a certain house, when I began to ask what I was to do out of boredom, a certain gentleman unknown to me, evidently not a Moscovite, suddenly turned to me and said with irritation: "Ah, take a piece of telephone wire and hang yourself to the first telegraph pole! There is nothing else left for you to do!"

Yes. And at night I begin to understand why I am so bored. Why then? Why? It seems to me, it is because of this. . . .

First, I know exactly nothing. Once I learned something, but, the devil take it, I either forgot everything, or my knowledge is of no use anywhere, and it seems that every minute I stumble upon a discovery of America. For example, when they tell me that Moscow ought to be canalized, or that cranberries do not grow on a tree, then I ask in surprise, "Really?"

From my birth I have lived in Moscow, but by the Lord,

I don't know where Moscow came from, why it is, for what object, for what reason, what good it is. In company, at table, I make a fuss with the others about city-economy, but I don't know how many versts there are in Moscow, how great a population it has, how many are born and how many die, how much we earn and how much we spend, the extent of our trade and with whom we carry it on — which city is wealthier: Moscow or London? If London, then why? But every fool knows it! And when in company some question comes up, I shudder and am the first to begin to shout, "Let it be submitted to the Committee! To the Committee!"

I grumble with the merchants that it is time Moscow established trade with China and Persia, but we don't know where this China and Persia can be found, and whether they need anything except water-soaked, worm-eaten little cheeses. From morning to night I munch at Lyestov's restaurant, and don't myself know why. I play a part in some kind of play, and don't know what the play is about. I go to see "The Queen of Spades" and only when they have already raised the curtain, I remember that I, it seems, have not read Pushkin's story, or have forgotten it. I write a play and produce it, and only when it falls through with a crash, do I realize that exactly such a play has been written before, by Vl. Alexandrov, before him by Fedotov, and before Fedotov by Shpazhinski. I know neither how to speak, nor to argue, nor how to carry on a conversation. When in society somebody speaks to me about something unknown to me, I simply act the knave. I assume a sad, mocking expression, seize hold of

. my companion's coatbutton, and say: "That, my friend, is old," or, "You contradict yourself, my dear fellow. . . . At leisure we will somehow settle this interesting question and come to an agreement, and now tell me, for God's sake, did you attend the performance of 'Imogene'?"

When they speak in my presence, for example, about the theatre and the modern drama, I understand nothing but when they put their question to me, it is not hard for me to answer: "That is so, gentlemen, . . . Let us suppose, everything is so. . . . But then, where are the ideas? Where the ideals?" Or even, drawing a deep breath, I shout, "Oh, immortal Molière, where are you?" Or, waving a hand impressively, I go to another room. There is another fellow Lope-de-Vega, a Danish dramatist, I think. So with him also I sometimes stupefy the public; — "I will tell you as a secret," I whisper to the company, "that that phrase Calderon borrowed from Lope-de-Vega." And they believe me. . . . Go and find out!

Because of the fact that I know nothing I am not at all cultured. It is true, I dress in the fashion, have my hair cut at Teodor's, and my home is elegantly furnished; nevertheless I am an Asiatic and *mauvais ton*. I have a four-hundred-dollar writing-table, with inlay work, plush furniture, pictures, carpets, busts, a tiger skin, but the vent in the oven is stuffed up with a woman's jacket, or there is no spittoon, and I, as well as my guests, spit on the carpet. On my staircase there is the odor of frying goose; my lackey has a sleepy face, the kitchen is dirty and foul-smelling, while under the bed and the chests of drawers are cobwebs, dust, old boots, greenish mold, and

papers that smell of the cat. Things are always at sixes .
and sevens: either the stove smokes, or the rooms are cold,
or the casement-window does not close, or, in order that
the snow may not blow into the study-window, from the
street, I hasten to stuff a pillow into the opening. It also
sometimes happens that I live in furnished rooms. You lie
on the divan in your room and think of your boredom,
while in the adjoining room, on the right, some German
woman fries cutlets on a kerosene-burner, and on the left
some girls bang on the table with empty beer bottles.
From my room I study "life," see with accurate vision
everything that goes on in the furnished rooms, and write
only about the German woman, about the girls, the soiled
napkins, describe drunkards and brutalized idealists, and
conclude that the most important question is that of the
lodging houses and the intellectual proletariat. Yet, truly,
I observe nothing. I am very easily reconciled to low
ceilings, and roaches, and dampness, to drunken friends
who throw themselves down on my bedding without re-
moving their dirty boots. Neither pavements spread with
yellow-brown dirt, nor dirt-heaped corners, nor offal-cov-
ered gates, nor misspelt signboards, nor ragamuffin beggars, — nothing offends my æsthetic sense. On the narrow sleigh of the *izvoschiks* I have squeezed myself in like
a ghost, the wind pierces me through and through, the
izvoschik lashes me about the head with his whip, the
wretched little horse is barely able to drag itself along, —
but I don't notice this. It is all the same thing to me!
They tell me that the Moscow architects, instead of houses,
built a kind of soap-boxes and spoiled Moscow. But I

don't find that these boxes are bad. They tell me that our museums are fitted out poorly, ignorantly, and uselessly. But I don't visit the museums. They regret that Moscow has only one well-arranged picture-gallery, and that even this one was closed by Tretyakov. Closed! Well then, so be it. . . .

But let us turn to the second reason for my boredom: it seems to me that I am unusually clever and important. When I go visiting, when I speak, or remain silent, or read about literary things, or eat to bursting at Lyestov's, — I do all these things with the greatest aplomb. There is not an argument which I don't enter into. It is true, I don't know how to speak, but on the other hand, I know how to smile ironically, shrug my shoulders, shout. I, an ignorant and uncultured Asiatic, am in the main content, but I create an impression of being content with nothing, and this I do so cleverly, that at times I even believe it myself. When they give something funny at the theatre I want very much to laugh, but I hasten to give myself an appearance of serious concentration; if, God, forbid, I should smile, what would my companions say? If someone behind me laughs I look around sternly, — an unfortunate lieutenant, one other like Hamlet and like me, becomes confused, and, as if excusing himself for his sudden laugh, says: "How vulgar! What a show-booth!"

And in the entracte I say out loud at the buffet, "The devil knows, what a play! It is revolting!" "Yes, a mere farce," replies some one, "but, do you know, it is not without an idea." . . .

"Oh come now! That motif has long ago been worked

up by Lope-de-Vega, and, of course, there can be no comparison! But how dull! How oppressively boring!"

At the performance of "Imogene," because of having to suppress a yawn, I almost dislocate my jaws, my eyes pop out of my head for boredom, my mouth is dry, . . . but on my face is a smiling, blissful expression.

"Here is consolation," I say in an undertone. "I have not had such lofty pleasure in a long, long time!"

Sometimes I want to play and disport a bit at a music hall; and I would gladly cut loose, and I know that in a time of dejection it would be very salutary, but — what will they say in the editorial rooms of *The Artist?*

No, God preserve me!

At an exhibition of paintings I usually wink, shake my head significantly, and say in a loud voice, "It seems to me everything is there: plenty of spirit, expression, and color, — but the principal thing, — where is the idea? Where is that? What expresses the idea here?"

In regard to the journals, I demand honesty, no matter whether the articles be written by professors or by residents of Siberia. Whoever is not a professor, or has not been to Siberia, that man cannot have genuine talent. I demand that M. N. Ermolov treat only of ideal girls, not over twenty-one years old; I demand that classical plays be produced at the Little Theatre exclusively by professors. . . . Absolutely! I require that even the most unimportant actors, before they venture on the stage, should acquaint themselves with the literature about Shakespeare, so that, when the actor says, for example, "A quiet night,

Bernardo!" everyone may at once feel that he has read eight volumes.

I often, very often, have things printed. As recently as yesterday I went to the editors of a thick journal to inquire whether my novelette would come out (56 printed pages). "Truly, I don't know how it will be," said the editor, confused, "it is really, you know, very long, and, — uninteresting."

"Yes," I say, "but, on the other hand, honest!"

"Yes, you are right, agrees the editor, still more confused. "Certainly, I will publish it." . . .

The girls and ladies of my circle are also unusually clever and important. They are all alike; they dress alike, speak alike, walk alike, and the only difference is that one has heart-shaped lips, while the other, when she smiles, has her mouth wide like that of a turbot.

"Did you read Protopopov's latest article?" the heart-shaped lips ask me. "It is a revelation!"

"And you, of course agree," says the mouth of a turbot, "that Ivan Ivanich Ivanov,* in his passion and strength of conviction, reminds one of Belinski. He is my consolation."

I confess, *she* came to see me. I remember very well our declaration of love. She sits on the divan. Her lips are heart-shaped. Horridly dressed, "without pretense," a foolish coiffure; — I put my arm round her waist, — her stays crack, — her cheek is salt.. She is abashed and flurried, embarrassed. "Forgive me," she says, "how can one reconcile honest conduct with such vulgarity as love?

----

* The author Jones, or Smith.

What would Protopopov say if he should see? Oh, no, never! Leave me! I offer you my friendship!" But I say that friendship alone is not enough. Then she threatens me coquettishly with her finger, and says, "Good, I will love you, but on condition that you hold the banner high."

And when I hold her in my embrace, she whispers, "We will struggle together. . . ."

Then, living with her, I learn that the vent in her stove, too, is stopped with a woman's jacket, and that under her bed, too, the papers smell of the cat, and that she enters into arguments in the same way, and at art-exhibitions, like a parrot, gabbles about atmosphere and expression. And she also, must have an idea! She drinks vodka secretly, and, on retiring, smears her face with sour cream, to look younger. There are roaches in her kitchen, dirty washcloths, a stench; and the cook, when she bakes pastry, before placing it in the oven, scratches the upper crust with a comb taken from her hair, and, in preparing pies, moistens the raisins with her mouth in order to make them stay more firmly in the dough. And I run! Run! My romance flies to the devil, and *she*, the important one, the clever one, squeaks everywhere, "He has changed his convictions!"

The third reason for my boredom is, — my violent, excessive envy. When I am told that somebody or other has written a very interesting article, that somebody's play has been successful, that J. won 200 thousand, and that N.'s speech produced a profound impression, I squint knowingly, I become altogether cross-eyed, and say, "I am very glad for his sake, but, then, you know, in '74 he was tried for theft!"

My soul turns into a piece of lead; with all my being I hate him who has been successful, and I continue:

"He tortures his wife, and has three mistresses, and is forever giving dinners to the critics. In general he is a real beast. . . . The story is not bad, but without a doubt he stole it somewhere. His want of talent cries to Heaven. . . . Indeed, to speak frankly, I find nothing in particular in the story. . . ."

On the other hand, suppose somebody's play has failed, I am tremendously happy, and hasten to take the author's side. "No, gentlemen, no!" I cry. "There is *something* in the play. At all events, it is literary."

Do you know, everything base, mean, abominable, that is said of persons of any note, was circulated throughout Moscow by me? Let the city-head know that if he has successfully built, for instance, a good pavement, I will feel a hatred for him and will spread the rumor that he robs wayfarers on the highroad! If someone tells me that a certain newspaper has already gained 50,000 subscribers, I will begin to say everywhere that it is subsidized. Another's success, — for me it means shame, humiliation, a heart-sore. . . . What talk can there be here of social, civil, or political feeling? If ever I had such feeling, envy has long since destroyed it.

Thus, knowing nothing, uncultured, very clever, and unusually important, consumed by envy, with an enlarged liver, yellow, gray, bald, I prowl from house to house, give the tone to life, and everywhere bring something yellow, gray, bald. . . .

"Ah, what boredom!" I say in a despairing voice. "What oppressive boredom!"

I am as infectious as influenza. I bewail my boredom, give myself airs, and from envy calumniate my friends and neighbors; but see, — some student in his teens lends an ear, runs his hand through his hair, importantly, and throwing the book aside says, "Words, words, words, — God, what boredom!" He squints, he too becomes like me, and repeats, "Our professors are now delivering lectures for the benefit of the famine-stricken. But I am afraid that they will put half of the money into their own pockets."

I prowl about like a shade, do nothing, my liver grows and grows. . . . And meanwhile time flies, I am becoming old and weak; you will see, — some day I shall fall ill with the influenza and die, and I shall be dragged to Bagankov;* for a time I will be remembered by two or three of my friends, and they will forget me, and my name will cease to be even a sound. . . . We live our life only once, and if you have not lived in the days that were given you, then count them as lost. Yes, lost, lost!

And meanwhile I could have learned and known everything; if I had gotten rid of the Asiatic in me, I might have studied and loved European culture, commerce, trade, village economy, literature, music, painting, architecture, hygiene; I might have built a good pavement in Moscow, trade with China and Persia, diminished the death-rate,

---

* Burial-ground.

combated ignorance, corruption, and all the abominations that hinder us so when we try to live. I might have been reserved, courteous, cheerful, kind-hearted; I might have rejoiced over every success of others, since, however small, every success is already a step towards happiness and truth.

Yes, so I might! So I might! But I am a foul rag, trash, sour fruit; I am a Moscow Hamlet. Carry me away to Bagankov!

I toss about under my bed-cover, from side to side, am unable to sleep, and always keep wondering why I am so bored, and until morning there sound in my ears the words: "Take a piece of telephone wire, and hang your-self to the nearest telegraph-pole! There is nothing but that left for you!"

Printed first in the Russian newspaper, Novoe Vremya, Dec. 7, 1891, under the pseudonym of "Kislyaev."

ANTON CHEKHOV'S DIARY
1896-1903

THE DIARY

1896 - 1903

My neighbor V. N. S. told me that his uncle Fet-Shenshin, the famous poet, when driving through the Mokhovaia Street, would invariably let down the window of his carriage and spit at the University. He would expectorate and spit: Bah! His coachman got so used to this that every time he drove past the University, he would stop.

In January I was in Petersburg and stayed with Souvorin. I often saw Potapenko. Met Korolenko. I often went to the Maly Theatre. As Alexander [Chekhov's brother] came downstairs one day, B. V. G. simultaneously came out of the editorial office of the *Novoye Vremya* and said to me indignantly: "Why do you set the old man (i. e. Souvorin against Burenin?" I have never spoken ill of the contributors to the *Novoye Vremya* in Souvorin's presence, although I have the deepest disrespect for the majority of them.

In February, passing through Moscow, I went to see L. N. Tolstoy. He was irritated, made stinging remarks about the *décadents*, and for an hour and a half argued with B. Chicherin, who, I thought, talked nonsense all the time. Tatyana and Mary [Tolstoy's daughters] laid out a patience; they both wished, and asked me to pick a card out; I picked out the ace of spades separately for each of them, and that annoyed them. By accident there were two aces of spades in the pack. Both of them are extraordinarily sympathetic, and their attitude to their father is touching. The countess denounced the painter Gé all the evening. She too was irritated.

May 5. The sexton Ivan Nicolayevitch brought my portrait, which he has painted from a photograph. In the evening V. N. S. brought his friend N. He is director of the Foreign Department. . . editor of a magazine. . . and doctor of medicine. He gives the impression of being an unusually stupid person and a reptile. He said: "There's nothing more pernicious on earth than a rascally liberal paper," and told us that, apparently, the peasants whom he doctors, having got his advice and medicine free of charge ask him for a tip. He and S. speak of the peasants with exasperation and loathing.

June 1. I was at the Vagankov Cemetery and saw the graves there of the victims of the Khodinka [During the coronation of Nicholas II in Moscow hundreds of people were crushed to death in the Khodinka Fields.] I. Pavlovsky, the Paris correspondent of the *Novoye Vremya,* came with me to Melikhovo.

August 4. Opening of the school in Talezh. The peasants of Talezh, Bershov, Doubechnia and Sholkovo presented me with four loaves, an icon and two silver salt-cellars. The Sholkovo peasant Postnov made a speech.

N. stayed with me from the 15th to the 18th August. He has been forbidden [by the authorities] to publish anything: he speaks contemptuously now of the younger G., who said to the new Chief of the Central Press Bureau that he was not going to sacrifice his weekly *Nedelya* for N.'s sake and that "We have always anticipated the wishes of the Censorship." In fine weather N.

walks in galoshes, and carries an umbrella, so as not to die of sunstroke; he is afraid to wash in cold water, and complains of palpitations of the heart. From me he went on to L. N. Tolstoy.

I left Taganrog on August 24. In Rostov I had supper with a school-friend, L. Volkenstein, the barrister, who has already a house in town and a villa in Kislovodsk [in the Caucasus]. I was in Nakhichevan — what a change! All the streets are lit by electric light. In Kislovodsk, at the funeral of General Safonov, I met A. I. Tchouprov [a famous economist], later I met A. N. Vesselovsky [littérateur] in the park. On the 28th I went on a hunting party with Baron Steingel, passed the night in Bermamut. It was cold with a violent wind.

2 September in Novorissisk. Steamer *Alexander II.* On the 3rd I arrived at Feodossia and stopped with Souvorin. I saw I. K. Aivasovsky [famous painter] who said to me: "You no longer come to see me, an old man." In his opinion I ought to have paid him a visit. On the 16th in Kharkov, I was in the theatre at the performance of "The Dangers of Intelligence." 17th at home: wonderful weather.

Vladimir Soloviov [famous philosopher] told me that he always carried an oak-gall in his trouser pocket, — in his opinion, it is a radical cure for piles.

October 17. Performance of my "Sea-gull" at the Alexandrinsky Theatre. It was not a success.

29th. I was at a meeting of the Zemstvo Council at Sezpukhovo.

On the 10th November I had a letter from A. F. Koni who says he liked my "Seagull" very much.

November 26th. A fire broke out in our house. Count S. I. Shakhovsky helped to put it out. When it was over, Sh. related that once, when a fire broke out in his house at night, he lifted a tank of water weighing 4½ cwt. and poured the water on the flames.

December 4. For the performance [of the "Seagull"] on the 17th October see "Theatral," No. 95, page 75. It is true that I fled from the theatre, but only when the play was over. In L.'s dressing-room during two or three acts. During the intervals there came to her officials of the State Theatres in uniform, wearing their orders, P. — with a Star; a handsome young official of the Department of the State Police also came to her. If a man takes up work which is alien to him, art for instance, then, since it is impossible for him to become an artist, he becomes an official. What a lot of people thus play the parasite round science, the theatre, the painting, — by putting on a uniform! Likewise the man to whom life is alien, who is incapable of living, nothing else remains for him, but to become an official. The fat actresses, who were in the dressing room, made themselves pleasant to the officials — respectfully and flatteringly. (L. expressed her delight that P., so young, had already got the Star.) They were old, respectable house-keepers, serf-women, whom the masters honored with their presence.

December 21. Levitan suffers from dilation of the aorta. He carries clay on his chest. He has superb studies for pictures, and a passionate thirst for life.

December 31. P. I. Seryogin, the landscape painter, came.

1897.

From January 10 to February 3 busy with the census. I am enumerator of the 16th district, and have to instruct the other (fifteen) enumerators of our Bavykin Section. They all work superbly, except the priest of the Starospassky parish and the Government official, appointed to the Zemstvo, G., (who is in charge of the census district); he is away nearly all the time in Serpukhovo, spends every evening at the Club and keeps on wiring that he is not well. All the rest of the Government officials of our district are also said to do nothing.

With such critics as we have, authors like N. S. Lyeskov and S. V. Maximov cannot be a success.

Between "there is a God" and "there is no God" lies a whole vast tract, which the really wise man crosses with great effort. A Russian knows one or other of these two extremes, and the middle tract between them does not interest him; and therefore he usually knows nothing or very little.

The ease with which Jews change their religion is justified by many on the ground of indifference. But this is not a justification. One has to respect even one's indifference, and not change it for anything, since indifference in a decent man is also a religion.

February 13. Dinner at Mme. Morosov's. Tchouprov, Sololevsky, Blaramberg, Sablin and myself were present.

February 15. Pancakes at Soldatienkov's [a Moscow

publisher]. Only Golziev [editor of *Russian Thought*] and myself were present. Many fine pictures, nearly all badly hung. After the pancakes we drove to Levitan, from whom Soldatienkov bought a picture and two studies for 1,1000 roubles. Met Polyenov [famous painter]. In the evening I was at professor Ostroumov's; he says that Levitan "can't help dying." O. himself is ill and obviously frightened.

February 16. Several of us met in the evening in the offices of *Russian Thought* to discuss the People's Theatre. Every one liked Shekhtel's plan.

February 19. Dinner at the "Continental" to commemorate the great reform [the abolition of the serfdom in 1861]. Tedious and incongruous. To dine, drink champagne, make a racket, and deliver speeches about national consciousness, the conscience of the people, freedom, and such things, while slaves in tail-coats are running round your tables, veritable serfs, and your coachmen wait outside in the street, in the bitter cold — that is lying to the Holy Ghost.

February 22. I went to Serpukhovo to an amateur performance in aid of the school at Novossiolki. As far as Zarizin I was accompanied by. . . . a little queen in exile, — an actress who imagines herself great; uneducated and a bit vulgar.

From March 25 till April 10 I was laid up in Ostroumov's clinic. Hæmorrhage. Creaking, moisture in the apices of both my lungs; congestion in the apex of the right. On March 28 L. N. Tolstoy came to see me. We spoke of immortality. I told him the gist of Nossilov's story "The

Theatre of the Voguls," and he evidently listened with great pleasure.

May 1. N. arrived. He is always thanking you for tea and dinner, apologizing, afraid of being late for the train; he talks a great deal, keeps mentioning his wife, like Gogol's Mijniev, pushes the proofs of his play over to you, first one sheet then another, giggles, attacks Menshikov, whom Tolstoy has "swallowed"; assures you that he would shoot Stassiulevitch, if the latter were to show himself at a review, as President of the Russian Republic; giggles again, wets his mustaches with the soup, eats hardly anything, and yet is quite a nice man after all.

May 4. The monks from the monastery paid us a visit. Dasha Moussin-Poushkin, the wife of the engineer Gliebov, who has been killed hunting, was there. She sang a great deal.

May 24. I was present at the examination of two schools in Tchirkov. [The Tchirkov and Mikhailovo schools.]

July 13. Opening of the school at Novossiolki which I have had built. The peasants gave me an icon with an inscription. The Zemstvo people were absent.

Braz [painter] does my portrait (for the Tretiakov Gallery). Two sittings a day.

July 22. I received a medal for my work on the census.

July 23. In Petersburg. Stopped at Souvorin's, in the drawing-room. Met VI. T. . . . who complained of his hysteria and praised his own books. I saw P. Gnyeditch and E. Karpov, who imitated Leykin showing off as a Spanish grandee.

July 27. At Leykin's at Ivanovsk. 28th in Moscow. In the editorial offices of *Russian Thought,* bugs in the sofa.

September 4. Arrived in Paris. "Moulin Rouge," danse du ventre, Café du Néon with Coffins, Cafe du Ciel, etc.

September 8. In Biarritz. V. M. Sobolevsky and Mme. V. A. Morosov are here. Every Russian in Biarritz complains of the number of Russians here.

September 14. Bayonne. Grande course landoise. Bull-fight.

September 22. From Biarritz to Nice via Toulouse.

September 23. Nice. I settled into the Pension Russe. Met Maxim Kovalevsky; lunched at his house at Beaulieu, with N. I. Yurassov and Yakobi, the artist. In Monte Carlo.

October 7. Confession of a spy.

October 9. I saw B.'s mother playing roulette. Unpleasant sight.

November 15. Monte Carlo. I saw how the croupier stole a louis d'or.

1898.

April 16. In Paris. Acquaintance with M. M. Antokolsky [sculptor] and negotiations for a statue of Peter the Great.

May 5. Returned home.

May 26. Sobolevsky came to Melikhovo. Must put down the fact that, in Paris, in spite of the rain and cold, I spent two or three weeks without being bored. Arrived

here with M. Kovalevsky. Many interesting acquaintances: Paul Boyer, Art Roë, Bonnie, M. Dreyfus, De
Roberti, Waliczewsky, Onieguin. Luncheons and dinners,
at I. I. Schoukin's house. Left by Nord-express for Petersburg, whence to Moscow. At home, found wonderful
weather.

An example of clerical boorishness. At a dinner party
the critic Protopopov came up to M. Kovalevsky, clinked
glasses and said: "I drink to science, so long as it does no
harm to the people."

1901.

September 12. I was at L. Tolstoy's.

December 7. Talked to L. Tolstoy over the telephone.

1903.

January 8. "Istorichesky Vestnik," November 1902,
"The Artistic Life of Moscow in the Seventies," by I. N.
Zakharin. It is said in that article that I sent in my
"Three Sisters" to the Theatrical and Literary Committee.
It is not true.

Printed in the United States
145393LV00002B/26/A

9 781432 575724